Routledge Revivals

Stalin's Russia

First published in 1940, *Stalin's Russia* is a close study of the development of the Stalinist regime and the flaws in socialist doctrine that made it possible.

The book examines the contrasts between the "free and equal" society heralded by the Marxist-Leninist programme and the totalitarian state that emerged in its place. It makes use of a wealth of material to cast light on the inner workings of Stalin's regime. It explores the significance of the Stalin-Hitler pact, and argues that the word "socialism" itself became a liability to any genuine movement of liberation as a result.

Stalin's Russia

And the Crisis in Socialism

By Max Eastman

First published in 1940
by George Allen & Unwin

This edition first published in 2021 by Routledge
2 Park Square, Milton Park, Abingdon, Oxon, OX14 4RN
and by Routledge
605 Third Avenue, New York, NY 10017

Routledge is an imprint of the Taylor & Francis Group, an informa business

© 1940 Max Eastman

All rights reserved. No part of this book may be reprinted or reproduced or utilised in any form or by any electronic, mechanical, or other means, now known or hereafter invented, including photocopying and recording, or in any information storage or retrieval system, without permission in writing from the publishers.

Publisher's Note
The publisher has gone to great lengths to ensure the quality of this reprint but points out that some imperfections in the original copies may be apparent.

Disclaimer
The publisher has made every effort to trace copyright holders and welcomes correspondence from those they have been unable to contact.

A Library of Congress record exists under LCCN: 40027209

ISBN 13: 978-0-367-75224-8 (hbk)
ISBN 13: 978-1-003-16155-4 (ebk)
ISBN 13: 978-0-367-75222-4 (pbk)

Book DOI: 10.4324/9781003161554

STALIN'S RUSSIA

AND

THE CRISIS IN

SOCIALISM

by

MAX EASTMAN

London
GEORGE ALLEN AND UNWIN LIMITED

FIRST PUBLISHED IN GREAT BRITAIN
IN 1940
Copyright in the U.S.A.

*Printed in Great Britain by
Billing and Sons Ltd., Guildford and Esher*

CONTENTS

FOREWORD 7

PART ONE

THE FAILURE OF THE RUSSIAN REVOLUTION

1. THE END OF SOCIALISM IN RUSSIA 17
2. THE MEANING OF THE MOSCOW TRIALS 52
3. STALIN BEATS HITLER TWENTY WAYS 81
4. THE DEATH AGONY OF AN IDEA: 95
   AN OUTLINE OF THE COMINTERN
5. TROTSKY'S DIVORCE OF ENDS AND MEANS 120
6. THE MOTIVE-PATTERNS OF SOCIALISM 128

PART TWO

SOCIALISM RECONSIDERED

7. THE PREDICAMENT OF THE WORD "SOCIALISM" 149
8. SOCIALISM AS PHILOSOPHY OR SCIENCE 161

CONTENTS

9.	DEFECTIVE BLUE-PRINTS	173
10.	TRUTH IN THE MARXIAN WORLD-VIEW	197
11.	THE ROLE OF PERSONALITIES	210
12.	THE DOCTRINE OF CLASS STRUGGLE	215
13.	WHAT TO DO NOW	243
	INDEX	267

FOREWORD

This book is the fruit of long and anxious study, first of Marx's theoretical philosophy, second of Lenin's impetuously practical application of it, third of the gradually developing results of the revolutionary experiment set going under Lenin's guidance.

I never thought the Marxian philosophy scientific, and I had begun to formulate my objections to it in some articles in the old *Masses* long before the Russian revolution. When I went to Russia in 1922 to study the Bolshevik experiment at first hand, I found this philosophy established as a state religion and bowed down to on all sides with Byzantine obsequiousness. This seemed to contrast strangely with the intensely practical, experimental, and in many ways skeptical, good sense of Lenin. I was enamored of that practical good sense. I thought Lenin's heretical way of going at the conquest of power and the building of socialism a great deal more scientific than orthodox Marxism. I thought too that orthodox Marxism, enthroned as a state religion, was impeding the progress of Lenin's effort. It seemed to me the most important contribution I could make would be to criticize the philosophy, and show that Lenin's mode of procedure was a departure from it in the direction of scientific method.

Instead of writing a Soviet travelogue, therefore, while I was in Russia and after, I wrote a theoretical book called *Marx and Lenin, the Science of Revolution*. Part I is a criticism of the Marxian system, in which I would make but few changes today. Part II is an exposition, and endorsement, of the science of revolutionary engineering which Lenin based upon, or evolved out of, Marx. That too, so far as the exposition goes, still seems valid to me. But I think, in the light of subsequent results, that my endorsement of it was a mistake. I am not sure but that Lenin, if he were alive now, and saw how far crude human nature has run away with his soviet structure and militarized party led by "professional revolutionaries," would conclude that there must have been some fundamental error in his method.

To me, at any rate, as the criminal tyrannies of Stalinism have piled up—and of fascism and Nazism too—their connection with that wonderfully practical system of "revolutionary engineering" invented by Lenin has grown more and more obvious. It was indeed practical as a system for seizing power and overthrowing the rule of the bourgeoisie. But from that point on, it was utopian. It trusted too much in education, too much in the reasonable and kind and tolerant and freedom-loving qualities of human nature. Or more accurately, perhaps, it trusted too much in the benign intentions of a dialectic universe. Lenin really believed that his revolutionary power-machine would "die away" after its work was done. He believed that all power-machines, all organs of compulsion, the state itself, would "die away."

Even while endorsing his system, I did not share that belief. I did believe, however, that a socialization of land and capital would "transform the instruments of production, which serve today mainly to enslave and exploit labor, into simple instruments of labor freely associating." I agreed that the proletariat, being the lowest class in society, "could not emancipate itself without emancipating all society." I thought, as all socialists did, that there would be less government, that there would be more liberty and more individuality, as well as a true equality of opportunity, after that act of collectivization, which would make everybody a proletarian, and eliminate the whole business of rent, profit and interest. I believed essentially in education, and I thought that education only needed that chance. Since I fell for all these things without the support of a benignly dialectic universe, I might perhaps be condemned as more gullible than the orthodox Marxians, not less so.

At any rate I was gullible. I thought that bourgeois democracy was something once for all achieved, something we could afford to kick out from under us as we took the further step toward industrial democracy. I thought that the degree of independence achieved by men under the bourgeois democratic regimes was more prized by them, or prized by more of them, than it is. I have learned from Stalin's Russia and Hitler's Germany and Mussolini's Italy how much infantile and primitive savage yearning for dependence, for external authority, for the sovereign-father, there is in the average human heart. The political institutions, and still more important, the social habits, of democracy are in danger now, and I am for defending them on all fronts. Whether in a revolutionary crisis, or in more desultory struggles, I think they should be regarded, not as a step to transcend, but as a foundation to build upon. I am no longer willing to throw away my own liberties on the theory that I haven't any. And I feel the same way about the liberties, however qualified by economic strangulation, which are indubitably possessed in democratic countries by the masses of mankind.

As late as March 29, 1930, I was still praising and defending Lenin's organizational system. In a speech to the Foreign Policy Association I said:

"The Russian communist party is not like any organization that ever existed anywhere in the world before. It combines the essential features of a professional association, a scientific society, an ethical brotherhood, an army and a political party in the modern sense. Moreover, the composition of this organization, and therefore its equilibrium in the general population, is determined by drawing certain proportions from all the different economic classes of which society is composed. And moreover again, these proportions are altered from time to time according to the particular phase which the experiment is deemed to be passing through. Besides that, the party is surrounded by a whole group of graduated organizations which lean on it, and whose relations to it, both psychological and legal, are adjusted so subtly that it is not a figure of speech but a fact that this party extends its roots clear down to the politically unconscious bottom layers of society. It was by means of this subtle and altogether new political instrument which he created, and which he progressively adjusted with a sublety no outsiders dream of, that Lenin brought it about that when he seized the power and said he was seizing it in the name of the masses, he really was seizing it in the name of the masses, and although he held it in his single hand, all the powers in the world could not overthrow him."

Nothwithstanding this enthusiasm for the method, I was already troubled about the results. I continued:

"The Russian communist party, which now contains over a million members, occupies a position in the Soviet society similar to that occupied by the tsar under the old regime. The relation of its members to the different classes of society, and more particularly their relation to each other within the party, is the essential political question. It is the question of the location of the sovereignty. It is just here that I think the political situation in the narrow sense is unsatisfactory. . . ."

There the chairman stopped me. But from that point —helped on by Stalin's butcheries, and Hitler's employment of the same system for an opposite end—my thoughts traveled steadily. They were helped on also, I must acknowledge, by the heroic conduct of the democratic socialists in Vienna in February 1934, and of the Asturias miners in October of the same year. When "yellow" socialists manned the barricades in defense of the democracy they believed in, and "reds" abandoned the armed revolution they believed in at a shout from the dictator, it became easier for those whose hearts had been with the "reds" to think with their minds only about the two beliefs.

I now think that this brilliant device for engineering a seizure of power, invented by Lenin with a superdemocratic purpose, has shown itself to be in fatal conflict with the purpose. I think that an armed seizure of power by a highly organized minority party, whether in the name of the Dictatorship of the Proletariat, the Glory of Rome, the Supremacy of the Nordics, or any other slogan that may be invented, and no matter how ingeniously integrated with the masses of the population, will normally lead to the totalitarian state. "Totalitarian state" is merely the modern name for tyranny. It is tyranny with up-to-date technique. And the essence of that technique is a reverse use of the very thing upon whose forward action Lenin ultimately relied, the machinery of public education.

I put this much of my book in the introduction, because it seems to me that when a person changes his mind upon a basic question, he ought to state the fact, and make the nature of the change explicit both to himself and others. Much unnecessary confusion results from the habit intellectuals have of pretending when they learn something that they knew it all along.

Max Eastman

JANUARY, 1940

PART ONE

The Failure of the Russian Revolution

1

THE END OF SOCIALISM IN RUSSIA

It was a strange experience, for one who had lived through these twenty-five years as a Marxian socialist, to see how in proportion as the Soviet regime dropped overboard one by one every vestige of socialism, the liberal scholars and littérateurs of the whole world, in so far as they were at all flexible, "came over" to socialism, and rallied with extreme emotion to the "defense of the USSR." Maxim Gorky, Romain Rolland, George Soule, Waldo Frank, Rockwell Kent, Malcolm Cowley, Sidney and Beatrice Webb, Harold Laski—the list could be extended indefinitely of those representative intellectuals who, having remained cold to the efforts of the Bolshevik party under Lenin and Trotsky to establish a workers' and peasants' republic, substantially swallowed down "Marxism" as soon as the official "Marxism" ceased, either within the Soviet Union or anywhere else, to mean business about working-class power, or contain any fighting threat to the existing distribution of wealth.

It was a strange experience, and for one who rests his final hope upon human intelligence, a sad one. A prime factor in the wisdom of Karl Marx was his perception of the discrepancy between the ideas with which men commonly make and write history and the actual forces in play, the actual changes that are in progress. He called these loose-floating ideas *ideologies,* a term of contempt which he borrowed from Napoleon Bonaparte, and which freely translated into American means "applesauce." And he made heroic efforts to delve down under all ideologies and use his mind in the making of history as a mechanic does in the making of bridges or automobiles. It was by using his mind in this ardently matter-of-fact way that Lenin guided the Russian workers' and peasants' revolution to victory and laid what seemed to be the foundations of socialism.

Since Lenin's death, ideology has prevailed in the ruling circles and the controlled press of Soviet Russia to the practical exclusion of scientific straight-thinking about society and politics. The assertions that they are "building a classless society," and yet more that "socialism is finally and irrevocably achieved in the Soviet Union," are but crowning instances of this process of universal self-deception, samples of a particularly sublime "applesauce" under cover of which the exactly opposite process is in full flight—the restoration of class privilege and the soaking out of the foundations of socialism. To my mind there is not a hope left for the classless society in present-day Russia. Inside of ten years, barring revolutionary changes, the Soviet Union bids fair to be as reactionary as any country which has emerged from feudalism.*

THE CULTURAL REACTION

In the summer of 1934 I wrote an article saying every good thing that I could find to say of the socialist experiment in Russia. The theme of my article was that in that country, because of the socialization of industry and the removal of class privilege, progress hitherto considered utopian was being made "in every sphere in which radical reformers and what we call dreamers are wont in our country to beat their brains out against a cold rampart of cynicism and indifference." I supported this by quoting our own leading authorities who had gone there and seen what was being done, each in his own special field of interest—education, prison reform, public health, women's freedom, sex and family relations, birth control, prostitution, yellow journalism, drug addiction, alcoholism, rights of national minorities, elimination of anti-Semitism, mental hygiene, administration of justice, peace, war and patriotism, economic planning. My thesis was that the proprietary enjoyment of wealth by a priv-

---

* This chapter was written in the spring of 1936 and first published as an article in *Harper's Magazine*, January 1937. Some of its statements may seem too moderate now.

ileged few is what blocks progress on all these fronts and makes the efforts of truly social-minded idealists in capitalist countries all but futile.

I intended to follow my article with another saying the bad things that from the same standpoint an honest mind must say about the Soviet Union—chiefly, that these blessings of achievement, and yet more of hope, had been accompanied by a concentration of political power and privilege in the hands of a bureaucratic caste supporting an autocrat more ruthless than the tzars had been. I intended to point out that this situation, hateful in itself, was also a mortal danger, and if continued, certain death to the whole system. But I was still asserting the existence of the system.

After writing the first article, however, reading it to a group of friends, and showing it to one editor, I put it away in my desk as an anachronism. The conditions it described were disappearing while I wrote. Of the fundamental ones, those three which stand in most vital relation to the property system and the future—education, women's freedom and the family, peace, war and patriotism—there is now little but a memory and a clinging to the memory left.

In my section about education, I quoted from Miss Lucy Wilson, who made her pilgrimage to Russia in 1925 and stayed to 1927, and from John Dewey, who followed her a year later, such ecstatic testimony to the liberation of Russian schools and children from socially irrelevant and spirit-killing regimentation that they sounded like another *News From Nowhere*. "Almost incredible to me, an eye-witness," said Miss Lucy Wilson. And John Dewey: "I cannot convey it; I lack the necessary literary skill."

These utopian conditions were founded upon manifestos and decrees of the Lenin government adopted shortly after the seizure of power, containing phrases such as these:—

"Pupils of the older classes in the secondary schools, must not, dare not, consider themselves children, and govern their destiny to suit the wishes of parents and teachers. . . . Utilization of a system of marks for estimating the knowledge and conduct of the pupil is abolished. . . . Distribution of medals and insignia is abolished. . . . The old form of discipline which corrupts the entire life of the school and the untrammeled development of the personality of the child, cannot be maintained in the Schools of Labor. The process of labor itself develops this internal discipline without which collective and rational work is unimaginable. . . . All punishment in school is forbidden. . . . All examinations—entrance, grade and graduation—are abolished. . . . The wearing of school uniforms is abolished."

All this was swept from the earth, letter and spirit, by a "Decree on Academic Reform," issued by the Stalin government on September 4, 1935, and by instructions following it, of which the following phrases will convey the drift:—

"Instruct a commission . . . to elaborate a draft of a ruling for every type of school. The ruling must have a categoric and absolutely obligatory character for pupils as well as for teachers. This ruling must be the fundamental document . . . which strictly establishes the regime of studies and the basis for order in the school as well as the rules of conduct of pupils inside and outside of school. . . . Introduce in all schools a uniform type of pupils' report card on which all the principal rules for the conduct of the pupil are to be inscribed. Establish a personal record for every pupil. . . . Every five days the chief instructor of a class will examine the memorandum, will mark cases of absence and tardiness in it, and will demand the signature of the parent under all remarks of the instructor. . . . Underlying the ruling on the conduct of pupils is to be placed a strict and conscientious application of discipline. . . . In the personal record there will be entered for the entire duration of his studies the marks of the pupil for every quarter, his prizes and his punishments. . . . A special apparatus of Communist Youth organizers is to be installed *for the surveillance of the pupil inside and outside of school*. They are to watch over the morality and the state of mind of the pupils. . . . Establish *a single form of dress* for pupils of the primary, semi-secondary, and secondary schools, this uniform to be introduced to begin with, in 1936, in the schools of Moscow. . . ." [Italics mine.]

Needless to dwell upon the difficulty I experienced in basing an argument upon John Dewey's raptures of 1928, when such a back-jump to the complete temper of education under tzarism—spiritual prison uniforms, political surveillance and an—was already in the wind.

In the sphere of sex and family relations, or, in other words, upon the problem of the freedom and rights of woman and the related problem of population control, the counter-revolution in the Soviet Union in the past two years * has been so crudely put over that even our serenest ideologues become uneasy in their dreams of "building socialism in one country." Everybody who means business about socialism in any country knows that a stoppage of the pressure of population on the means of subsistence is essential to the beginnings of it. In a country like Russia, where mothers in hundreds of thousands are unable to produce, or buy, milk for their babies, and the problem of homeless children is openly acknowledged to be unsolved even in the capital, to come out with a proclamation advocating—or more accurately, decreeing—large families and wholesale human breeding, is not only remote from socialism, but from sane human kindness and sound reason in any of its forms. It is the madness of military nationalism in a power-clique which looks upon the masses of the population as its cattle and its cannon fodder.

It is needless to remark that the "holy instinct of motherhood" has once more come into its own as a weapon of this reaction (*Pravda,* May 28, 1935), and

* 1935-36.

also the proposition that "woman having received rights has therewith received duties" (*Pravda*, June 7, 1935)— a conception of "rights" known only to those whose permanent prerogative it is to give and withhold them. It is somewhat more surprising to see "chivalry," and not only "chivalry" but "knightliness"—a word of bitter execration to all Russian revolutionists for a century— now solemnly brought forward in the cause of woman's re-enslavement. We learn that, having accepted the above duties as well as rights, woman has "put man under the obligation to care for her with special knightliness." And this new knightliness is thus defined: "Every girl must be treasured not only as a textile worker, a bold parachute jumper or an engineer, but as a future mother. The mother of one child must be treasured as the future mother of eight." (*Pravda*, June 7, 1935.) Just how far the mother of eight children will go as an engineer or a parachute jumper, is well known to those who use their brains when they think.

To give teeth to this reactionary decree, and make clear that it relates only to the ill-paid masses of the workers and the peasants, it is enforced by raising the costs of divorce and alimony beyond the reach of these human cattle, and making abortion, one of woman's few real guarantees of liberty, once more a crime. That it will not be a crime to those who have money and are in the know—those most particularly who issue the decree—

is perfectly well understood by all who understand anything. It is class legislation and discriminatory sex legislation in its foulest form. It is the absolute end of that utopian reign of freedom, justice, and mature intelligence upon all questions relating to sex and family relations which led Cicely Hamilton, returning from her pilgrimage to Moscow in 1933, to report "the most important advance . . . which has been made since the race developed from brute to human."

As to the foundation laid by Lenin of a revolutionary policy and high public temper upon the problems of peace, war, and patriotism, there is not the shadow of it left. Even in my article I was compelled to point into the past for this. It was on May 29, 1934, that Litvinov announced in Geneva that the Soviets would abandon their anti-war alliance with the workers and oppressed peoples of the earth, and play the game of military diplomacy with the capitalist nations. It was not long after that Stalin himself issued a joint statement with the French premier Laval in which he "fully approved the national defense policy of France in keeping her armed forces on a level required for security." To "vote war credits," even after a world war began, was the crime of treason to Marxian principle which caused Lenin to abandon the Second International and the word "socialism," and form a Third for which he took the uncorrupted term "communism" from the banners of the civil wars of 1848. In the name of Lenin, the Third International now supports the armies of imperialistic governments in time of peace. Having handed the power to Hitler without shaking a fist, this "Leninist" organization makes Hitler a pretext to enter again the old system of military alliances which turned Europe in Lenin's eyes into "one bloody lump." And to bathe this change in the appropriate emotions, *Pravda,* the official organ of Lenin's party, hauls down the Marxian banner, "Workers of the world unite!" and runs up the slogan of all mad dogs of war: "Defense of the fatherland is the supreme law of life." Let us taste a few sentences from *Pravda's* editorial of June 9, 1934:—

"For the fatherland! That cry kindles the flame of heroism, the flame of creative initiative in all fields in all the realms of our rich, of our many-sided country. . . .

"For the fatherland! That cry raises tens of millions of toilers to the defense of their great fatherland and puts them in fighting readiness.

"Millions and tens of millions of people acclaim in our brave fliers great patriots of their fatherland, for whom the honor, glory, might and prosperity of the Soviet Union is the supreme law of their lives. . . .

"The defense of the fatherland is the supreme law of life. . . .

"For the fatherland! For its honor, glory, might and prosperity."

Compare that with the language of Lenin:—

"The essential thing is for us to be, even when times are most trying, real internationalists in deed. . . .

There is one and only one kind of real internationalism: hard work at developing the revolutionary movement and the revolutionary struggle in one's own land, and support (by propaganda, sympathy, material aid) of such, and only such, struggles and policies in every country without exception."

Compare the two and you have a measure of the change since Lenin died.

And if you want a measure of the extremes to which ideology can go where criticism is stifled, you need only be informed that the above affirmation of universal hysteric passion for the fatherland was the preface to a decree—printed immediately below it—making it a crime of treason to "escape over the border" of this same fatherland, and punishing this crime by "shooting and confiscation of all property." Moreover, if it is a soldier who thus "escapes abroad"—for "abroad" and "over the border" are the same word in Russian—the grown members of his family who knew of his intention and did not notify the police, so that he could be shot before he went, get five to ten years in prison with confiscation of property; and those *who did not know of it,* but lived with or were supported by him at the time of his contemplated act, may be "deprived of citizenship and exiled for five years to a remote region of Siberia."

It is only necessary to add that this abandonment of every vestige of Lenin's policy of socialist internationalism has been followed by a reorganization of the army on the Western plan, abolition of the militia system, restoration of the titles, ranks, and privileges of officers, and revival of the uniforms and special rights of Cossack troops.

I need not go through the whole index of my utopian article, and examine to what extent the cultural counter-revolution has affected each one of those ideal reforms, or manifestations of unfettered social intelligence, upon which I was proposing to base so grand an argument. These three are vital—education, sex and family relations, and the stand on peace and war. With high intelligence abrogated in these spheres, we can cherish few extreme hopes in others. Whether my argument is abstractly valid or not, it no longer applies to the Soviet Union.

POLITICAL TYRANNY

The fact that these reactionary decrees are being issued on the theory of a "complete triumph of socialism" in the political and economic spheres, and on the plea that what is oppressive in a capitalist society is progressive under socialism, that what is tyranny here is freedom there, merely reveals the degree to which critical thinking about real facts has been supplanted by ideology, honesty by crude deception.

In the spring of 1935 Stalin's government issued a decree which made the death penalty for theft—adopted for adults three years before—applicable to minors from the age of twelve. When this fact was announced at a congress of the French Teachers' Federation in August of the same year, the Stalinsts in the Federation indignantly denied it. Being shown a copy of *Izvestia* (April 8, 1935) containing the decree, they lapsed into silence, but they were ready next day with the information that "under socialism children are so precocious and well educated that they are fully responsible for their acts"! It is but a reflection of the manner in which this ideology is being stretched to cover every saddest thing in Russia.

In view of such a decree, one blushes almost to recall that according to Marxian theory the state as an "instrument of compulsion" was supposed to "die away" with the triumph of socialism, and this process was to begin the very moment the industries of a country were socialized. This minor detail has been so far forgotten by the adherents of Stalin that they themselves boast in the same breath that socialism has "completely and irrevocably triumphed" and that Stalin heads "the strongest government on earth." When confronted with this inconsistency, they explain it by alluding to the "capitalist encirclement." But that did not trouble them when assuring us in 1925 that "socialism" could be built in one country.* They were already talking ideologies and not facts.

The words "socialist" and "communist" are changing their meaning just as the word "Christian" did. Just as heretics were burned by thousands in the name of the love of the neighbor, so peasants have been starved by millions in the name of the workers' and peasants' republic. The crude animal egoisms of men and classes of men thus grab ideas and use them, not as heroic lights to action, but as blinds to hide inaction or actions that are too base. Lenin abandoned the word "socialism" because it had become a smoke screen for a policy of place-hunting and accommodation to capitalism, and seized the other word to cleanse and renew the idea of proletarian revolution. Stalin's ideologists have invented the scheme of making socialism mean a "first stage" in the development of communism, thus elaborating the smoke screen and making it possible to put over in the name of "socialism" policies of reaction that would horrify the

---

* There was no true disagreement about whether socialism could be built in one country. All sane and sincere communists, whether Stalinist or Trotskyist, wanted to build all the socialism they could in Russia—and how much they could, nobody knew. The issue was whether meanwhile Russia should abandon her alliance with the revolutionary working-class movements of other countries, or join her old imperialist allies in the game of military power. Had Trotsky been a less philosophical Marxist, or a more astute politician, he would never have been maneuvered into defending the negative side of an unreal question.

most conservative antagonists of Lenin, policies that, but for the smoke screen, would horrify enlightened opinion in every country of the globe. If your wayward child stood under the threat of being shot for theft at twelve, it would matter little whether he were shot on the theory that property has been "socialized" and now belongs to everybody.

When you remember that Marx placed at the very basis of his system the assertion that the proletariat, being the lowest class in society, could not emancipate itself without emancipating all mankind, and described socialism in consequence as "the society of the free and equal," you see how deep is the degeneration of this term. Within the same year Walter Duranty wrote an article describing Russia as a completely "regimented land" in which "the principle of state control over the lives of individuals has been fully and firmly established," and another article asserting that "the battle for socialism in the USSR is definitely won." You may cling, as a strict Marxian, to the opinion that this heartless tyranny has appeared in place of the promised freedom only because Russia is a backward country with an economy of scarcity to which, in isolation, socialist theory does not apply; or you may propose to revise the theory. But you cannot as a thinking socialist assent to this glib journalistic talk.

I have myself never been a sufficiently orthodox and trustful Marxian to believe in the happy legend of how men, once wealth-producing property is owned in common, will find themselves living together in natural cooperative brotherhood as angels live. It rests, more than most of Marx's judgments, upon the relics of Hegelian mystic metaphysics. I have been all the more keenly aware, however, that in the proposed new society the location of the sovereignty is the supreme political question, and that if power is permanently shifted from the rank-and-file of the working class and self-supporting peasants, organized in freely arguing and democratically controlled institutions, to a privileged and bureaucratic ruling caste, the experiment in socialism will not last long. And even from the standpoint of this more modest demand, you cannot say that politically the battle for socialism is "definitely won in the USSR." You must say, if you are talking straight facts, that the battle is definitely lost. The power has passed irrevocably—except by revolution—from the workers' and peasants' organization to the organizations of a privileged bureaucracy.

This process began long before Lenin died, and the fight against it, the fight for "Workers' Democracy" against bureaucratism, occupied his last months and days and hours as a leader. It was in the crises of this fight that he attacked Stalin as rude, disloyal, capricious, nationalistic, and spiteful *—as complete a characterization (if you change "rude" to "brutal") as history will ask—and recommended that he be removed from his position as General Secretary of the Party. Under Stalin's leadership the power has been withdrawn completely from the workers and peasants. The soviets have become but the relic of a rough draft of proletarian self-government. The power is in the hands of a dictator and an organization of bureaucrats, still called the communist party, but by continual abuse of "purges" and periodic "verifications of credentials" cleared and cleaned of every trace of independent act or even discourse questioning the ruling clique, or in clear terms denying the infallibility (which is little but the divine right) of the dictator.

Ella Winter, who ranks just above Louis Fischer and Anna Louise Strong as our most naïve ideologist of the "workers' republic," says on page 281 of her fervid book, *Red Virtue:* "All restrictions against intellectuals of bourgeois origin were abolished by Stalin in the speech of June 23, 1931." That is true. That is how Russia is governed—by speeches from the throne. And this shift of sovereignty, nurtured with unceasing vigilance since 1924, has reached its culmination in the new "demo-

* The citations will be found in my book *Since Lenin Died*, pp. 21 and 22, and in the document called "The Testament of Lenin" printed in the appendix to *The Real Situation in Russia* by Leon Trotsky.

cratic" constitution, which is nothing but a sweeping out of the refuse of workers' rule to make way for a totalitarian state not in essence different from that of Hitler and Mussolini. The prelude to this constitution was a dissolution of the "Society of Old Bolsheviks," and a reorganization of the "Communist Youth," raising their upper age limit to twenty-five, and at the same time, by a significant logic, removing them from all participation in politics! Its other prelude was the recent shooting of the old colleagues of Lenin—of which more later—and the simultaneous police clean-up of thinking Bolsheviks, called "Trotskyists" or "Zinovievists," in every branch of the Soviet existence, from the cotton harvest to the Kammerny Theater and the Astronomical Observatory. With these preludes in mind, let us examine the constitution.

On the plea that socialism is achieved and that there are no longer any classes in Russia, that we are now verily in the society of the free and equal, Stalin has dissolved, not the communist party and its monopoly of political action and organization, as one might expect from those exalted premises, but the soviets based on factories and the electoral superweight of the industrial workers—the sole relics left of the idea of a distinctly proletarian democracy, the sole things in the whole political set-up that really point to socialism. A glance through this "most democratic constitution in the world" is sufficient to show that its representational schemes are too complicated and too slow of movement to have efficacy in expressing the "will of the people" even if they formed the real structure of the state. Their contrary operation is indeed assured, as Albert Goldman has pointed out, by the retention of the bicameral system in which the upper chamber, like a House of Lords or Senate, being based on the functionaries of the various republics, forms an integral part of the bureaucratic apparatus, and has the power at any time of bringing about through "disagreement" a legal dissolution of them both. All socialists and all radical democrats have always opposed this super-parliament as a bulwark of privilege, even when it had not this power, and even where the two parliaments really formed the legislative state. The real state under Stalin's constitution is still to be the communist party, now nothing but a pyramid of bureaucrats supporting Stalin, who will operate this unwieldy "parliamentary" monster, and make it produce votes just as at the county fair a cardboard cow produces milk.

What is the "secret ballot" when only one party can run candidates for office, and that the party in power? What is "free press and assemblage" when no man can form, advocate, or support the platform of any but the gang in power, and when ten to twenty thousand * of

* Hundreds of thousands now.

those who have done so are in jail or exile while you talk about it? What is the whole talk under these conditions about how "we" are going to "*give* the Russian people" (*sic!*) the most democratic constitution on earth? Is there any term in the American language to describe it except "applesauce"?

Let us turn from this unedifying political sideshow—assassination of the phantom of proletarian democracy by the caricature of representative government—to the economic facts which underlie it.

ECONOMIC EXPLOITATION

Socialism means a classless society, and a classless society means that a privileged minority of the population are not in a position to enjoy the national wealth, while the majority live only in their labor to produce it. It means especially that privileged individuals who do have excess income cannot invest it in the instruments of production with which others work, thus reducing them to a position of fixed subservience. It means an end of rent, profit, and interest on stocks and bonds, an end of "surplus value," an end of the exploitation of labor. To all those other cultural goods of which we have been speaking, this economic change was regarded by socialists as prerequisite and fundamental.

That being the case, it is obvious that if Russia were a socialist state, or if its sovereigns had the slightest intention of allowing it to become one, we should know exactly what is the distribution of the national income among the different categories of the population and in what direction it is traveling. We should know how much of that income goes not only as salary, but in the form of unpaid privileges, to the captains of industry and office-holders of the state, trade unions, co-operatives, collective farms, and communist party. We should know how much of it is going to the payment of 7 and 8 per cent interest to the holders of government bonds and savings-bank books, who constitute not only a privileged caste, but to the extent of their holdings capitalists in the essentially important sense of the term. We know nothing accurately about all this, and for the very good reason that accurate statistics are of all things least compatible with the free proliferation of ideologies.

Even without these statistics we can glean enough to prove that when our recently Marxified liberals come home from a brief tour of the Soviets telling us how well "socialism works" in Russia, they are really only telling us that life there is not radically different for people of their class from what it is here.* Among the reassuring practicalities of life under the Soviets reported by

* They are telling us, too—and this is one of Stalin's truly subtle dispensations—that life is more luxurious for writers in Soviet Russia than it has ever been before in any place. General education has made publicity as important a weapon of despotism as the armed forces. In Soviet Russia the Fourth Estate has almost replaced the Second.

George Soule, for instance, a prominent place was occupied by the news that it had been found "necessary to stimulate enterprise and ability by differential rewards," and that "there is no resentment of the fact that some people dress better than others." That Mr. Soule in this particular voyage was not functioning as the keen-minded economist he is, may be seen in the fact that he reported no inquiry as to the magnitude of this "differential reward," or the degree of this difference of dress—how keenly it can be felt, for instance, by the peripheral nerve-endings in the long Russian winter. Here are a few figures as to this "differential reward"—figures gleaned from a studious scrutiny of matter printed in the Soviet press through inadvertence, or when those interested in the distribution of wealth were not supposed to be looking. I quote Leon Sedov, writing on the Stakhanovist Movement in *The New International* for February 1936:—

"There is hardly an advanced capitalist country where the difference in worker's wages is as great as at present in the U.S.S.R. In the mines, a non-Stakhanovist miner gets from 400 to 500 rubles a month, a Stakhanovist more than 1,600 rubles. The auxiliary worker, who drives a team below, gets only 170 rubles if he is not a Stakhanovist and 400 rubles if he is (*Pravda,* Nov. 16, 1935)—that is, one worker gets about ten times as much as another. And 170 rubles by no means represents the lowest wage, but the *average* wage, according to the data of Soviet statistics. There are workers who earn no more than 150, 120 or even 100 rubles a month. . . . The examples we give by no means indicate the extreme limits in the two directions. One could show without difficulty that the wages of the privileged layers of the working class (of the labor aristocracy in the true sense of the term) are 20 times higher, sometimes even more, than the wages of the poorly-paid layers. And if one takes the wages of specialists, the picture of the inequality becomes positively sinister. Ostrogliadov, the head engineer of a pit, who more than realizes the plan, gets 8,600 rubles a month; and he is a modest specialist, whose wages cannot, therefore, be considered exceptional. Thus, engineers often earn from 80 to 100 times as much as an unskilled worker."

The whole standard of living of the Russian people is extremely low by comparison with ours, and that helps our ideologues ignore the fact represented by this last figure. "The differences of income . . . ," says Edmund Wilson, "are, from the American point of view, very slight; but they are, for Russia, very considerable." The differences of salary, in so far as this figure reveals them, are alike in Russia and America. It is probably, as the author says, not an exceptional figure. But assuming that it is, let us compare it with exceptional American figures.

In the *New Republic* for July 15, 1936, there appeared a table comparing the salaries of officers in some of our wealthier American companies with the average weekly wage of the workers employed by them. I learn from this table, picking it up at random, that Mr. C. F.

Kelley of the Chile Copper Co. receives $50,600 a year, his average worker $23.58 per week—a difference of 1 to 41. Mr. George Horace Lorimer of the Curtis Publishing Co. has been receiving $90,500 a year and his average worker $33.68 per week—a difference of 1 to 51. If we take 170 rubles a month as the wage of a Russian worker—and being based on rather shamefaced statistics this is a very high estimate of the average—and compare it with the salary paid to Mr. Ostrogliadov, we have a difference of 1 to 50. We are evidently among the same magnitudes.

We need only assume that Mr. Ostrogliadov's laborers are for the most part unskilled, and receive the low but by no means unusual wage of 100 rubles a month, to see that his salary of 8,600 rubles compares favorably with that of Mr. H. F. Sinclair, an officer of Consolidated Oil, who receives an annual wage of $126,659 while his workers get along on $29.53 a week. The ratio here is 1 to 82. That in the case of Mr. Ostrogliadov, 1 to 86.

It is not necessary to carry the comparison farther in order to show that the "differential reward" under what is called "socialism" is not radically different, in so far as salaries are concerned, from that under American capitalism.*

---

* A decree of August 29, 1938, set an upper limit to salary payments of 2,000 rubles a month, except by special decree of the Council of Commissars. This would legalize under normal circumstances a "differential reward" of 1 or 2 to 20, and provide for such exceptional figures as those discussed above.

END OF SOCIALISM IN RUSSIA 41

The low level of all income in the Soviet Union is what makes life seem so different. According to recent official claims a ruble is worth twenty cents, and at that rate Mr. Ostrogliadov's salary would equal an annual stipend of $20,640 a year. Here again, however, official claims are optimistic; I doubt if the real salary, aside from "privileges," is much more than half of that. And this makes his "differential reward" seem, to people accustomed to regard such salaries as small, a significantly different thing from Mr. Sinclair's.

It is really in large part the backwardness of Russia that our literary tourists love. That medieval leisure and inviting of the soul, especially when combined with a childlike and eager enthusiasm for the beginnings of modernism, the joy of a national industrial birth and rebirth, is irresistible. They love Russia much as John Reed did when he went there *before the revolution*, and came home exclaiming: "Russian ideals are the most exhilarating; Russian thought the freest, Russian art the most exuberant; Russian food and drink are to me the best, and Russians themselves are, perhaps, the most interesting human beings that exist." * Our tourists link up these charms of an agrarian backwardness with the myth of a utopian leap into the future, and with the actual relics of the workers' republic, and become the

* Quoted by Granville Hicks in his *John Reed, the Making of a Revolutionary.*

more easy dupes of Stalin's ideology. They have that much excuse.

Last winter, at the time of her lecture in Los Angeles, I asked Anna Louise Strong, one who so loves Stalin's Russia that she "changed worlds" to be a part of it, whether it is true that Pilnyak, the novelist, received some years ago an annual income of 30,000 rubles a year —that is, some twenty to twenty-five times the present wage of an unskilled worker—and she answered, almost with asperity:—

"I don't know specifically about Pilnyak, but I dare say he does. I could, if I wanted to turn my mind to it."

I quote this to show how little Marx's idea of a society of the free and equal is really troubling these ideologues, and also because it adds one more drop of arithmetic to our conception of those "differential rewards." It casts a light, too, upon Harold Denny's dispatch to the New York *Times* of May 8, 1936, which appeared under the appropriate headlines: "Leisured Women Unite in Moscow"—"New Idle Class Gathers to Set Up Society to Help Workers Culturally"—"Aim Is to Make Life Brighter and Provide Useful Work for Executives' Wives."

Another American Stalinist recently returning from Moscow, to an inquiry after the health of Victor Vaksov, once head of the Metal Workers' section of the Red International of Labor, said: "He has done pretty well by

END OF SOCIALISM IN RUSSIA 43

himself. He is now head of one of the trusts in the automobile industry, has a fine house with two servants, two official cars at his disposal, and a Packard of his own bought in America." That is a significant statistic, when brought into relation to the thirty-odd dollars a month paid to metal-workers, and should be easy to verify.

For further statistical light I will quote this paragraph from a book on Soviet Russia, *The Revolution Betrayed*, by Leon Trotsky:—

"The real earnings of the Stakhanovists often exceed by twenty or thirty times the earnings of the lower categories of workers. And as for especially fortunate specialists, their salaries would in many cases pay for the work of eighty or a hundred unskilled laborers. In scope of inequality in the payment of labor, the Soviet Union has not only caught up to, but far surpasses the capitalist countries!"

The Stakhanov movement, it should be emphasized, is not only the adoption of American and German methods of labor organization and efficiency. It is the building up of a new privileged caste, an aristocracy of labor, who together with the highly paid foreman and managers can be relied on to support the dictator.

With the same disregard of the real aims of socialism, the "collectivization of agriculture" is being turned into a governmental grant of special privileges to vast corporations prospering at the expense of the masses of the peasants. Nothing could exceed the brutality, caprice, and disloyalty to socialism with which Stalin has handled this problem of problems. Expropriating the well-off peasants called "kulaks" at the point of the bayonet, shipping them to Siberia in cattle cars by hundreds of thousands, herding the remainder into collectives before even the machinery for large-scale farming was manufactured, he laid waste all fertile Russia like a battlefield. Then after a year or two he brought many of the deported "kulaks" trundling back and settled them on the farms with private allotments alongside for those still energetic enough to till them. And now he has turned the whole system into a reservoir of special privilege by granting the land "in perpetuity" to those collectives which, because of good soil, geographical location, etc., have signally prospered. That is, he has given away franchises to vast farming corporations, deeding them the hereditary right formerly possessed by the aristocracy to cultivate for their own profit the most fertile and advantageous portions of the Russian soil. It is hard to say whether this act is characterized more by irrelevant "caprice" or by systematic "disloyalty" to socialism. It is a consistent step only in the building up of social support for a Bonapartist clique.

Trotsky for some reason fails to note what seems to me the meat of this whole situation—the fact, namely, that these happy beneficiaries of "the triumph of socialism," the overseers, specialists, bureaucrats, and labor and collective farm aristocrats, are able to invest their incomes, not, to be sure, in risky shares and debentures producing on the average if they are lucky 4 or 5 per cent of interest, but in government bonds which pay 7 per cent, or failing that, to deposit them in savings banks where they are exempt from both inheritance and income taxes, and earn 8 per cent of interest. Taking this into consideration, it seems clear that a large proportion of the capitalists of America could profitably change places with them, *if the general level of wealth in the two countries were equal.*

That our liberal scholars and littérateurs should be converted to a "socialism" of that kind is not surprising. I do not mean that there is any equivocation in their motive; and I must add that their zeal, industry, and devotion, like that of many of the party communists, afford one of the few signs of life in a sufficiently dead political landscape. But it is impossible for one who has accepted, even to the extent that I have, the Marxian view of the role of ideas in history, not to see that the change they are bringing about is etymological rather than economic. They are playing their part in the process of deluding mankind and themselves with another ideology—a "socialism" which means as little in real fact and action as "Christianity" does to a busy and prosperous Christian.

After making the remark quoted above about "differential rewards," Mr. Soule asks himself a pertinent question:

"Well, then, why do not the more successful get all the power and rob the less successful, just as in capitalism?"

And he makes this reply:—

"The answer is that their money does not give them any power over the system, since they cannot own factories, mines, farms, apartment houses, newspapers, radio stations, stores or railroads—any of the means of production. They cannot employ labor in business enterprises. There are no shares, debentures, private bond issues, stock markets or commodity exchanges. . . . They can buy government bonds or put their money in a savings bank. There was much pride in the growth of savings accounts this year. They can travel. Social pressure will not allow them, however, to live on their savings without working. . . ."

Omitting some minor matters, then, like a high inheritance tax and "social pressure" against loafing (both declining rapidly), the substantial difference between "socialism" and capitalism seems to be that under "socialism," instead of investing your money at your own discretion, and your own risk, you let the government invest it for you and guarantee you a 7 and 8 per cent return on your investment. That does indeed prevent the amassing of prodigious fortunes, and might be described as a kind of Populist or Bryanite utopia, so long as it may last. But it has very little to do with the gulf between the proletariat and the owning class as a whole, or with the aims of socialism. And just where Mr. Soule thinks that "social pressure" is coming from as these tax-exempt investments of private capital continue to pile up, is a mystery. It would be interesting to know what a Marxist of the vintage of 1935 thinks "social pressure" is.

That a noted economist, even of "bourgeois" training, could be so naïve once he thrusts his head into the mists of the Soviet ideology would be astonishing were it not for the example of Sidney and Beatrice Webb, who are supposed to know something about economics from a socialist standpoint. They state that there is no "unearned income" in the country, in the very same three lines in which they discuss the borrowing of money at stupendous rates of interest by a government which is a vast corporation owning and operating all industry.

"Inflation," they say, ". . . amounts to a disguised cut in everybody's wages, which has hitherto been regarded as an objectionable form of taxation, though one found to be less injurious in an equalitarian community, in which there is . . . an absence of incomes that are unearned. A preferential expedient to which the Soviet Government usually resorts is an internal loan."

I am no economist, but I think I am not crazy. And if I am not, then when a government which is running the industries and employing the labor of a country takes loans from people who have excess income, and pays those people 7 per cent interest on the loans, those people are not only receiving unearned income, but they are receiving surplus value derived from the exploitation of the country's labor. And when you add to these bondholders the "twenty-five million depositors" in the State Savings Banks, "encouraged by interest at the rate of eight per cent and by total exemption of deposits from income tax, inheritance tax, and various stamp duties"—I am still quoting the fabulous Webbs—you have a situation as remote from socialism, to say nothing of "communism," as anything that could conceivably be put across upon the most gullible mind as a cynical imitation of it.

If an American man of money gets an average profit of 5 per cent on his various investments he thinks he is doing passably well, and he submits, without any very steady cry of "socialism," both to an income tax and to an inheritance tax upon this unearned increment. Under "soviet communism" the man of money is guaranteed an income of 7 and 8 per cent on his investments, and it is exempt from both income and inheritance taxes. It would be hard to suggest, offhand, a neater system for re-establishing class divisions in a society in which they had been badly shaken up and were in danger of complete elimination.

It is of course somewhat more simple for the Soviet

state, if you conceive it as distinct from the holders of these bonds and bankbooks, to repudiate its obligations than it would be for a mass of private enterprises. A Stalin-minded critic of my article has even suggested that some such trick is being deliberately played upon the Russian people. "If you raise a man's pay and force him to take bonds in proportion, then put the bonds through a conversion, and finally devaluate the ruble with a prospect of cancelling the bonds altogether, it looks more to me like an extremely heavy tax faintly gilded with patriotism, than the establishment of vested class interest." People who can persuade themselves that a governmental clique which will swindle people in that raw fashion, destroying their plans, their hopes, their families, their life-structures by millions in order to run the state, are going to run it in the interest of the Brotherhood of Man and the Co-operative Commonwealth, have a determination to deceive themselves with which I do not know how to cope. Marx dismissed as utopian the idea that good men could be relied on to bring about socialism. A great many Stalinists have learned this so well that they actually believe bad men can be relied on to do it, if they are bad enough.

It seems obvious that if these rapidly mounting debts are *not* repudiated, then not only do exploitation and the class society remain, but all the basic problems of capitalism remain—the inadequate buying power of those who live on wages, the consequent lagging of distribution behind production, the cycles, the depression, and in the end the rage for foreign markets. The sole fundamental new thing left is the planning power in the hands of the state. This may prove a very fundamental thing. So long as the state is ruthless enough to let four to six millions of the population starve to death in order to build up foreign credit, as was done (it is now admitted privately) by Stalin's state in 1933, it will certainly be momentous. But from the standpoint of the revolutionary science, it will mean that once more the toiling masses have taken arms and fought upon the barricades and died for equal liberty, and once more they have received for their pains a new and more efficient system of class exploitation.

Note: Calvin B. Hoover, in his *Dictators and Democracies*, makes a comment on my discussion of Russian bonds which, coming from an expert on such matters and a very judicious one, I feel obliged to quote:

> "There can hardly be any denial . . . that the Soviet state has revived essentially the same sort of differentials in income which are enjoyed by Joe Louis and the corporation executive in a capitalistic economy. Factually, it is difficult to say whether or not there is substance to Max Eastman's charge that a *rentier* class is likewise being developed. Up to very recent times bond issues in the Soviet Union were certainly not so much a device for investment by which one lived from surplus, as they

were a device for lowering incomes for everyone. Everybody had a fixed amount deducted monthly from his wage or salary, which amount went in theory to buy a bond. The worker who bought the bond was not allowed to sell it. The money which was paid to the worker in interest in succeeding years merely meant that wages were that much lower than they would have been if it had not been necessary to pay interest out of the current product of industry. It would have made little difference if the Soviet government had in the beginning simply paid wages and salaries in an amount low enough to leave a surplus equal to the sums raised by the bond issues. It is perfectly true that the device of guaranteed returns on state bonds might be the means by which a *rentier* class could develop, but time alone will tell whether this is going to happen. I do not believe that it has occurred to an important degree as yet."

Perhaps the situation can be summarized adequately for the present by saying that a mechanism has been set up which, in case the national income increases sufficiently to make a classless society possible, will effectually guard against it.

2

THE MEANING OF THE MOSCOW TRIALS

It would have been clear long ago that the Russian revolution had failed were it not for Stalin's skill in manipulating public opinion. His counter-revolution has been the bloodiest in all history. Aside from the punitive expeditions against peasants, the campaigns of state-planned starvation, the war of extermination against thinking people generally, he has put to death more sincere and loyal party-militants than ever died before with the death of a revolution. His work makes that of the guillotine after the arrest of Robespierre look pale indeed. And yet because of his crafty guidance of the steam-roller and the machine of publicity, it required an open pact with Hitler's Germany to wake the world up to the fact that Thermidor was ended, that he was the man on horseback.

Stalin was trained as a "professional revolutionist"; that is why his counter-revolution shows so few amateur defects. He knows all the moves that can be made against him; he knows all the moves to make. He has used every trick in the repertory of demagogism in his colossal task of proving all loyal Bolsheviks traitors to the cause, and selling his personal tyranny to the public as the super-scientific beginnings of a millennium. And he has used one trick never thought of before—that of making distinguished batches of the old revolutionists "confess" publicly and in the face of death that *they* are the counter-revolution, he the sole loyal leader of the Party.

This hoax has had so massive a success, not only in Russia, where to question the confessions is itself a capital offense, but among free-judging intellectuals elsewhere, that it must be separately discussed by anyone who asserts—no matter with what economic facts to back him—that Stalinism is the counter-revolution. People read the plain words spoken in the face of death by men of sound mind, and are overweighed by the mystery: "If they did not commit the crimes confessed to, *why* did they say they did?"

I understand why, but the understanding is so bound up with my personal experience of the mentality of the consecrated Bolshevik that I find it difficult to explain to Western minds. If I were asked to state in the order of their importance the grounds of my sure knowledge that those "confessions" were concocted party lies, I should begin with one which no one else has mentioned: the words in which they were spoken. To a man unacquainted with Marxian theory and Russian Bolshevik ways of thinking based upon it, I suppose the dime novel twaddle in which these Bolshevik leaders tried to explain their abandoning the theory and tactics of Marx and Lenin and taking up with the rejected doctrines of the *Narodovoltzi* in their wildest forms, may seem plausible. Some people have no feeling for styles and modes of thought. But anyone who has, and who is also acquainted with the literature and history of the Russian revolution, can see in a dozen pages that these Marxists were not describing a change of principle and tactic in their own minds, but were reciting the plot of a melodrama prepared without regard to their minds. There is hardly an indication in the entire published report of either trial that any one of the defendants ever read Marx, associated with Lenin, or acquainted himself with the intellectual history of the Russian revolution.

It is conceivable that a highly trained Bolshevik leader, a lieutenant of Lenin, might go over, under stress of the new concentration of power, to the principles of the Left Social Revolutionaries and far beyond them. It is hardly conceivable that all of Lenin's lieutenants would. But let us suppose they did. They would justify themselves in a language and with a set of concepts as remote from those employed by the defendants in this trial as the prescriptions of a trained physician are from the jabber of a witch doctor.

MEANING OF MOSCOW TRIALS 55

The fact that their stories did not jibe with the facts, that they described a rendezvous in a hotel that no longer exists, a trip in an airplane that never flew, a meeting with Trotsky in Paris when Trotsky was in a remote corner of France, is wholly incidental. To anyone who knows their minds, it is obvious that they were performing a studied falsification from the first word to the last.

THE MEN

I not only know their minds and the traditions of the movement to which they belong, I knew many of them personally. To me they were not just outlandish names in a gruesome Russian novel, but real human beings with beliefs and feelings much like mine. Some of them were my friends.

I went to Russia in 1922 and lived there as a friend of the government for two years. I had been editor of the only American magazine which supported the Bolsheviks from the day they seized power—the magazine which sent John Reed to Moscow and printed his first articles describing a "Ten Days That Shook the World." That gave me a very good entree into the inner circles of Bolshevism—as good, I think, as anyone had who was not an actual delegate to the Communist International.

Radek I knew well, and I have the testimony in his own handwriting of his friendship for me. Serebriakov

I knew far better, and admired a thousand times more. A stronger-hearted, honester and braver man I never knew. Muralov was a hero in my eyes. He was a hero in the eyes of all Russia. A genial kind-hearted giant, he led the fight in Moscow that lasted some days after Petrograd was in the hands of the workers and soldiers. He was afterward commander of the Moscow military district—one of the biggest, morally as well as physically, and one of the best-loved of those who fought in the front line during the October days.

Piatakov I remember as a slim, gentle, highly intellectual, delicately organized, friendly person, quietly very firm in his own judgments, for he had an instructed as well as a thinking mind, but genially attentive to others. We went to the circus together one of the last Saturdays before I left Moscow. His being dragged out to death for an alleged betrayal of socialism comes poignantly home to me. I know that he was not only a fine, loyal and humane character, but a man who represented, as few others did besides Lenin, Trotsky and Rakovsky, the highest intellectual culture to be found in the Bolshevik party.

Another man I knew well enough to love was Budu Mdvani, recently executed with forty other Georgian Bolsheviks. He is one of the many—how many, who will ever know?— that refused to confess, and were shot behind closed doors. A big, broad-shouldered, powerful, jovial, prodigiously laughing, astonishingly handsome, veritable dynamo of a man, one of the well-loved friends of Lenin and Trotsky and everybody else who ever knew him, one of the gorgeous people of the earth, a "prince" if there ever was one, and vastly amused to be confused with little titled princes of the same name. Now he is swept down too. They are all gone, all the great Bolshevik party men, the true leaders—either dead or in prison on the way to death.

Bukharin appealed less to me intellectually than some of the others, because he seemed inadequate to his task of party "theoretician," being thoroughly tangled up in a pile of knowledge that was too big for him. But he was a man of delicate sensitivity—an artist of talent—and a man who had lived his whole life in devoted labor for the socialist ideal. He served Stalin most of the time in a kind of bewildered despair, and his arrest added a nightmare touch to those trials, self-vilifications and shootings of all in Russia whom I trusted.

Sossnovsky, *Pravda's* chief feature writer under Lenin, I was associated with in an effort to found a new Soviet magazine which should be less narrowly political, more catholic in scope, than any then existing. We talked together endlessly at the editorial meetings—for with characteristic Russian hospitality I was asked to join the staff of the new magazine—and I admired and liked Sossnovsky as well as anybody I met in Moscow. Another true man, courageous and brainy, he stood out for his principles and spent years in a solitary confinement prison in Siberia for refusing to renounce the program of the Left Opposition. He too is disgraced and dead now, although he never stood up in court and asked me to believe that he had become a depraved beast.

I do not believe it of any of them because I knew them too well. I would not feel logically impelled to believe it, even if their conduct in court were as much a mystery to me as it is to the uninitiated. For that is only one mystery. Those who try to believe in the truth of the "confessions" have two mysteries to explain. First, how did poised, trusted, loyal and intelligent revolutionists come to commit these criminal, immoral, inhuman, stupid and counter-revolutionary acts? And second, how did it happen that the mere fact of being arrested and held a period of time in isolation made them all repent, change their principles, and go out eagerly to vilify themselves in the eyes of the world and in history forever?

Is it not improbable that sixteen, and then again seventeen, men, having entered a desperate plot, and having got caught, would all behave in exactly the same way? That in itself, it seems to me, is so improbable as to be incapable of belief. And yet the way in which they all behaved is so unlike the usual behavior of men caught in a desperate plot that we should be astonished if we read it about one man.

THE POLITICAL SITUATION

The certainty which arises from my knowledge of the men is, of course, reinforced by my understanding of the political situation—and that, not as it appears to an American fellow traveler, but as it appears to Russian Bolsheviks, trained and molded in the struggle against Menshevik socialism. To them Stalin, in abolishing the soviet system of government in the name of "democracy," had gone over bag and baggage to the Mensheviks. He had destroyed the chief monument of the genius of Lenin, abandoned Lenin's principles, the principles of the Bolshevik party, and the whole political perspective of the October revolution. The same thing was true of his support of the "Popular Front" in the Spanish revolution. Popular Front is nothing but a Western name for what was called in Russia "Menshevism."

The soviet system of government was supposed, according to the designs of Lenin and according to Marxian theory, to endure until, with industry socialized and classes abolished, the state as an instrument of compulsion should dissolve and "die away" in a voluntarily cooperative communist society. All intelligent Bolsheviks knew this, and they knew it as you know the alphabet.

Stalin's assertion that he was replacing the soviets with a "democratic" government because classes were already abolished, would not go down with a loyal follower of Lenin, therefore, even if classes had been abolished, and even if the new government were democratic. Classes are not abolished in Russia except upon paper, and the new constitution is not democratic even on paper. On the contrary, it removes the last obstacle to the dictatorship of a *Fuehrer—Vozhd* is the Russian word—supported by a society of nationalistic bureaucrats which enjoys, just as the Black Shirts do in Italy and the Brown in Germany, a monopoly of political action and organization, and the constitutional right to form a controlling nucleus in every other organization that exists! Politically, even if there were no international problem, there is no mystery in a wholesale shooting of old Bolsheviks in connection with this change.

But Lenin's revolutionary theory was international. The Bolshevik policy was supposed to apply to every country of the globe. The Russian soviet state was supposed to take the lead in applying it. Russia was supposed to give aid to the fighting proletariat of the whole world, especially in whatever part of the world a revolutionary situation arose. Her aid was supposed to encourage the proletariat to form soviets and seize the power as was done in Russia, against all other parties, republican and royalist, civil and military, liberal and

Menshevik alike. Stalin gave a disastrously belated and fatally inadequate aid to the republicans and Mensheviks in the Spanish Civil War. He gave more aid, at least, than there is democracy in his constitution. But as the price of this aid he demanded that the Spanish government remain republican, that proletarian soviets should not seize power, that all socialist and working-class parties should indefinitely postpone the class issue and cooperate with the liberals.

It is that policy of postponing the class issue and "cooperating with the liberals" in a revolutionary situation upon which Lenin split with the Mensheviks in Russia, and thereby gave its essential meaning to the word "Bolshevism," and to the Bolshevik party its historic role and its triumph. Never mind whether you think this Menshevik policy is "sensible" or not. Lenin was an extreme revolutionary Marxist, the last man in the world, it may well be, that you would have thought "sensible." The international policy of the "Popular Front" was just as direct a sweeping out and trampling under foot of the work of Lenin, and of his principles, as was the abolition of the soviet state. That policy, too, could not be put through in Russia without a general clean-up of the loyal followers of Lenin. And these two policies, the abolition of the soviet government and the Popular Front, were but high points in that total surrender of the Bolshevik positions which I described in the previous chapter.

To this must be added the steady swelling of a wave of popular discontent following the national disaster of forced collectivization, a discontent which threatened the very existence of Stalin's government. Peasant uprisings, grumblings among the workers, disaffection in the army, made any political opposition within the Party dangerous to Stalin in an extreme degree. His theoretical opponents were being converted into leaders of a mass uprising, whether they would or no, an uprising which had perhaps little to do with the grounds of their opposition. That mass uprising made a monolithic party absolutely essential to the survival of his personal dictatorship. He had to put down little-leaders all over the country, and to accomplish that he had to have a treason trial of big leaders. And since the biggest leader of all was beyond his grasp, he had to implicate him in the crimes attributed to everyone he shot. Trotsky has been crowned with many revolutionary laurels, but none more expressive than Stalin's invention of a "Trotskyist treason plot" as the sole means— even with Trotsky in another hemisphere—of breaking once for all the force of the October revolution.

That was the political mechanism of those trials. That is why men were shot as "Trotskyists" who had long ago repudiated Trotsky, some of whom had retired from all political struggle and discussion. Stalin no doubt feared them as potential leaders of a revolt against him, knowing they could see through the official ballyhoo to the essential facts. He knew that they all considered him a mountebank-Marxist and a usurper, no matter what they thought of Trotsky, and no matter how many "capitulations" they might sign. There is little doubt that his stool-pigeons had caught them in the treasonable act of saying so; that was the factual basis for the arrests. But more than he feared the old leaders, he feared a new revolt of the rank-and-file. He needed these deaths in order to put it down. He needed a treason plot led by Trotsky as a pretext for a wholesale clean-up of all loyal and clear-sighted Bolsheviks, both old and young. If there is any political mystery here, it is only because so many influential people have found it convenient not to face the political facts.

THE CONFESSIONS

Aside, however, from the political situation, you had only to line up on a page the crimes and stupidities to which all these eminent men confessed, and summon a little hard sense, in order to know that you were reading bad melodrama and not history. They said in the first trial that they had been futilely conspiring for some six years to assassinate Stalin and other former comrades in a mood of "sheer spitefulness," out of a mere "thirst for power," in secret collaboration with Hitler's secret police, and this "without any political program"—without any idea or object, that is, but revenge and personal ascendancy.

In the second trial they added to these crimes the following: a conspiracy to wreck by industrial sabotage the worker's state which they had created, and to betray this state in war to fascist Germany and feudal Japan, a conspiracy with the heads of these reactionary nations to invade the "socialist fatherland" and overthrow the "socialist government," a promise to them in reward for this service of sections of the said fatherland comparable to the New England states and most of the land west of the Mississippi, and a further promise to engineer "mass exterminations" of the socialist workers, and to "spread disease germs" in the military forces of the "socialist fatherland."

These acts and projects might conceivably be true psychologically—although politically impossible—of one pathological character in a group of eminent and trusted men. They could not be true of all the big men of a party and an epoch. They could not be true of a whole high-minded government. And it is nothing less than the original soviet government that Stalin shamed in this way and exterminated together with the soviet system.

I think that some liberals gave credence to these fantastic tales because they still imagine there is something in the nature of "Bolshevism" which explains or mitigates such acts of depravity. The acts are criminal, bestial and degenerate from every standpoint, but they are worse, if that is possible, from the standpoint of Bolshevism than from that of ordinary sanity and morality. They are acts of absolute and wanton treachery—to self, to friends, to principles, to party, to the working class, and to humanity. Anyone who believed them must in sober judgment despair of and despise the human race.

Before explaining the confessions as I understand them, I want to mention the following facts:

In the spring of 1925 I published a book called *Since Lenin Died,* in which I exposed the inner party fight that Lenin had been waging against Stalin just before he died. I cited the letters in which Lenin accused Stalin of "nationalism," and of acting in critical situations out of mere "spitefulness." I stated the fact—subsequently confirmed by Zinoviev and by Lenin's wife—that one of Lenin's last acts was to write Stalin a letter breaking off all "comradely relations" with him. And I quoted some phrases from the document called "Lenin's Testament."

In the autumn of 1926 I published that "Testament"

in full in the New York *Times* and other leading newspapers throughout the world. It was a letter written by Lenin on his death-bed to his party, warning them against Stalin's excessive power and his possible abuse of it. It advised that he be removed from the office of General Secretary and replaced by someone less "rude" and "capricious" and more "loyal." The existence of this document was immediately denied by the Moscow authorities, and my text was denounced as a forgery by the Stalin communists in upward of seventeen languages for ten consecutive years. A brief time before the first of these treason trials, however, this "non-existent" document—omitting only those parts which contain praise for Trotsky—was published by the Soviet printing house. Passages from it, quoted at the time by the *Christian Science Monitor,* coincided verbatim with my text.

I mention these facts, not only because I hope they may enhance my credibility in what follows, but also because that Testament of Lenin contributes a small item to my explanation of the nature of the "confessions."

I find the explanation in four unusual things: the peculiar ethics of Bolshevism, which commits its adherents to a habit of class-loyal lying; the fact that the Bolshevik experiment had failed, and the equivocal way in which it failed; Stalin's penal code, which holds the immediate family of a political offender punishable for his crimes, whether aware of them or not; * and, finally, the passionately vindictive character of Stalin.

PARTY LYING

Those old Bolshevik chiefs were shot as traitors for the reasons I have given. They were the big men of the revolution, and they might have been shot by any counter-revolutionary dictator. But the scheme of making them promote the counter-revolution by a death-hour declaration that *they* were the counter-revolutionists, could hardly have arisen except in a party where loyalty to factual truth had already, on theoretical principles, been subordinated to proletarian party loyalty.

These theoretical principles go back to Lenin, and they go back to Marx, and they go back to the mystical sophistics of Georg Wilhelm Friedrich Hegel. In the mind of Lenin they were of course offset, not only by an impetuous honesty, but by an unwavering sense of the necessity that the working class should trust the Party and its leaders. Nevertheless, the principles were Lenin's, and these famous confessions were by no means the first "mighty and well-forged lies" to be solemnly recited by great Bolsheviks in obedience to a Resolution of the Central Committee of the Party. It was generally understood that personal predilections in the

* See page 27.

matter of honor, as well as life, ought to be sacrificed as "bourgeois," at that high word of command. Thus, although it was not their sole motive, I think it is indubitable that the majority of Stalin's victims made their "confessions" and went to their deaths with a feeling that as loyal soldiers of the Party they were justified, and, so to speak, redeemed by that Resolution of the Central Committee.

It is easy to confuse a man's mind—and his morals, too, if his principles are not exceedingly simple—by holding him in absolute solitude except for the pressure of certain strong and convinced personalities. And when that pressure is preceded by an application of the "conveyor system" of mental and physical torment,* it takes not only a robust, but a pugnacious nervous system to resist it. I imagine that the effect of such continued torment upon high-strung and sensitive types is to reduce them to an almost infantine condition. They become like broken-hearted children, longing only for a father or a mother—for someone, anyone, to *tell them what to do*. It is then that the friendly comrade, fellow-member of the beloved Party, can successfully advise them to make, for the sake of the Party, the false confession demanded by the Central Committee. It will deliver them from torment; it will permit them to die. It will permit

---

* Described with authority by W. G. Krivitsky in his book, *In Stalin's Secret Service*.

them to die with a feeling that they have loyally served the Party and the revolution to the end. It would be too simple to say these men were buying death with their false confessions, but it is far nearer the truth than to say they were trying to buy their lives. They could have had but the tiniest hope of life; they were in a condition in which death seemed a relief.

Types too robust and pugnacious to succumb to this process of breaking down—or in the language of the Ogpu, "splitting"—a character, were not tried in public. And there is not the slightest reason to suppose that they were tried in private. As Krivitsky points out, for every *one* of the old Bolshevik leaders who "confessed," *one hundred* were shot behind closed doors.

POLITICAL CONFUSION

Even those weaker ones who did confess would probably not have done so had their political opinions been simple. It is difficult for a man to say that the cause to which he gave his whole life has failed. It is especially difficult when he gave it in a religious belief that the process of all history and Being Itself were on his side. There is no room for ultimate failure in the Marxian system. From any situation it is always only a question of finding the "way out for the proletariat." Besides that, in certain main points of its prospectus the revolution had not failed. In the basic matter of expropriating the private capitalist it had, however dreadfully, gone forward under Stalin. The Russian industries and even the Russian farms were collectivized. State planning was a fact; production was increasing; the workers were not unemployed on a large scale. Superficially considered, or measured in mere quantity, a major part of the socialist program seemed to have been enacted. Only the dynamic essence and the expected result were lacking. The power was in the wrong hands; it was a dictatorship of Stalin, not of the working class. And there was, by the same token, no sign whatever of economic freedom and equality. The working class was still enslaved and still exploited.

In these circumstances, would it be a simple thing to call Stalin's dictatorship the counter-revolution? It would, perhaps, if you had not given your life to produce it. It would, if you had something besides anarchy and a relapse to private capitalism with which to replace it. These old Bolsheviks had tried fitfully to displace it. They had at least talked vigorously about getting rid of "the bureaucracy," and restoring power to the workers. They had talked about Trotsky's cogent criticisms. But they could find no way. Trotsky himself, to tell the truth, has found no way. He advocates that the workers overthrow the bureaucracy which has resulted from the overthrow of October, but he does not suggest how this new overthrow is to be prevented either from restoring capitalism or from producing a new bureaucracy. No, these old Bolsheviks were confronted with but one alternative: either to pronounce their life work a failure, or to admit that there was *some hope* for socialism and the workers in the regime, or after the regime, of Stalin. They expressed it in their private conversation, which you may be sure was faithfully Marxian, by saying: "There is no *way out* except through Stalin."

This equivocal and complex condition of their minds made it easier for their wills to weaken in the long months of solitude, and the long hours of torment in the inquisition chambers of the Ogpu. They would not have made these confessions if Stalin had restored capitalism to Russia. He confused them, and the whole world, by modeling his counter-revolution on the fascist states.

PHYSICAL AND MENTAL TORMENT

I have used the word "torment" instead of "torture." Torture would leave its marks, and would fail to make sure of the victim's conduct in court. Even as it was, two of the victims, Smirnov and Krestinsky, did attempt to repudiate in public the testimony they had signed in secret. Had they been merely cowed by torture and the threat of its renewal, any one of them might have screamed out the truth when brought into a public place. They were not *cowed* by what they went through, but *convinced*—brought into a condition where they themselves believed in the necessity to close the ranks of the Party by confessing that their own opposition to Stalin had been a monstrous conspiracy, criminal and depraved. When Krestinsky's conviction weakened, and he did cry out in court, asserting that his confession was false and had been forced from him, it was, I feel quite sure, the other defendants, his comrades in capitulation, who gathered round him in the prison and persuaded him to go back the next day and carry through the program as agreed upon.

Although I substitute the word "torment" for "torture," it is of importance to realize that threats to their families, and the hope of saving those they loved from destruction, played a role in this torment. In this connection the treason law I spoke of is crucial. According to the law and custom of the "socialist fatherland," all those living in the same house or apartment with a man guilty of treason, are punishable by imprisonment and exile. My very reliable friend, Mrs. Wutherspoon of Pasadena, California, told me that on a visit to Moscow shortly after the first treason trial she called upon the wife of a world-famous Russian, a woman occupying a high position in a Soviet welfare institution. Mrs. Wutherspoon asked this woman her opinion as to the guilt of Kamenev, Zinoviev and the others. Her answer to the direct question was noncommittal, but she added: "Whatever may be the case with them, something ought to be done about their wives and children. Nobody knows where they are—they have disappeared from the earth." Kamenev himself revealed in court that a concern about the future of his children was the principal human thought in his mind. Krivitsky reports a rumor that Zinoviev gave as his two reasons for confessing, the fact that there was no other "way out" except with Stalin, and a concern for the safety of his family. Bargains were undoubtedly struck in some of those secret conferences of the old Party chiefs in the Lubianka prison, and although weakened by an almost universal doubt of Stalin's honor, clemency for the family would be the strongest thing he had to offer.

To sum it up: the men who confessed were sensitively organized intellectuals, reduced by solitary confinement and torment, and despair of any other political course for the revolution, to a condition in which they would accept the advice and instruction of their comrades to die as traitors in order to preserve the unity of the Party under Stalin. It is to be hoped that with the passage of time a more intimate light will be shed upon this problem. For my part, I feel very sure that it will only fill up with concrete details, or vary with individual exceptions, the above generalization.*

STALIN'S REVENGE

There still remains, however, one thing unexplained. There remains something extravagant to a point suggesting the madhouse in the statements these men coolly

---

* I do not mean to exclude the possibility that a chemical, as well as a physical and psychological third degree may have been employed in some of these cases. Walter Duranty himself said that Serebriakov "spoke as if half asleep, and his voice sounded strangely dreamy—everybody noticed it." After all, it is not a long step from castor oil to more specific remedies. Aldous Huxley gave the prescription some time ago in his essay on Writers and Readers:—

"A cachet," he says, "containing three-quarters of a gram of chloral and three-quarters of a milligram of scopolamine will produce in the person who swallows it a state of complete psychological malleability, akin to the state of a subject under deep hypnosis. Any suggestion made to the patient while in this artificially induced trance penetrates to the very depths of the subconscious mind and may produce a permanent modification of the habitual modes of thought and feeling.

"In France, where the technique has been in experimental use for several years, it has been found that two or three courses of suggestion under chloral and scopolamine can change the habits even of the victims of alcohol and irrepressible sexual addictions. A peculiarity of the drug is that the amnesia which follows it is retrospective; the patient has no memories of a period which begins several hours before the drug's administrations.

"Catch a man unawares and give him a cachet; he will return to consciousness firmly believing all the suggestions you have made during his stupor and wholly unaware of the way this astonishing conversion has been effected."

That might serve at least to make educated people skeptical of confessions extorted in prison. However, as a general explanation of these confessions it is both improbable and unnecessary. Physical solitude and psychological pressure and torment are enough. Most men can, in proper conditions and in due time, be made to "confess" to anything.

made. If Stalin were actuated solely by a political motive, would he not compel them to recite some story that people of realistic common sense might believe? He is far too shrewd to set these eminent statesmen out there before the public and give them *carte blanche* in telling anything *but* the truth.

That is why I say that Stalin's passionately vindictive character is a third element essential to a solution of the problem. Stalin was not content with shooting his former comrades who went against him, and he was not content with disgracing them and getting a political endorsement from them. He must also have revenge for all the galling things that had been said about him by them, and by all the less "rude" and "capricious" and more "loyal" Bolsheviks from Lenin down.

His revenge was to compel them to take upon themselves the guilt which they had imputed to him—sheer "spitefulness," mere "thirst for power," the lack of "any program" except personal ascendancy, and "disloyalty" in its most monstrous forms.

I think it is no accident that Stalin published Lenin's "Testament" at the very moment of the first treason trial. It was the sting of that supreme injury that he was wiping off. But his victims had also to assume the taint of certain "mass exterminations" of which he had been more recently and as justly accused.

I am supported in this hypothesis by the memory of

a conversation I had with one of Stalin's most courageous victims, Leonid Petrovich Serebriakov. When he was in this country with Amtorg in 1929 Leonid Petrovich came often to my house, and even met and talked with me in public, although, owing to my defense of Trotsky and my translations of his writings, I was something of a plague spot to other emissaries of the Soviet government.

I commented on this once, and Serebriakov answered me in two ways. He said:

"I am not afraid of anything. Don't you see that I can't cringe or slink? Look at my back." He got up and turned around. "My muscles won't work that way."

And then he added, in an altered tone:

"Besides, it doesn't make any difference what I do. Stalin will get me in the end, anyway. If he lives long enough he will get every single one of us who has ever injured him in speech or action. That is his principal aim in life. He is completely dominated by vindictive passion. He will lie back and wait ten, twenty, thirty years, secretly plotting to achieve an exquisitely appropriate revenge upon an enemy, and then when everything is ready he will spring. Believe me, I am not telling fairy stories. I have lived with him, roomed with him, camped with him on the battlefield. He is the most vindictive man on earth."

Serebriakov then told me the story, which I had

MEANING OF MOSCOW TRIALS 77

already heard from another source, and which Trotsky has repeated in the press, of how Stalin in a gathering of comrades who were discussing their idea of a perfect day said: "Mine is to plan an artistic revenge upon an enemy, carry it out to perfection and then go home and go peacefully to bed."

Serebriakov had a young daughter whom he loved better than any other thing, or person, or idea. So it seemed to me when he spoke of her, and other friends have said this of him. Although I never saw her, she is in the photograph that he left with me when he returned to Russia. For her sake, perhaps, he would "cringe and slink." For nothing else, I can honestly believe, that this world contains.

THE LESSON TO BE LEARNED

There is a momentous lesson to be learned from these Moscow confessions, and it can be learned only by those who see clearly what differentiates them from other forced confessions. It is the fact that the victims had no principled objection to dying with a lie upon their lips. They had only to be reduced to believing that it was a revolutionary lie, that the Party demanding it was still the Party of the proletarian dictatorship. When you reflect that thousands of supposedly critical intelligences in western Europe remained convinced of this fact even after the execution of the Party's leaders, it can hardly surprise you that some of them, by such a process as I have described, could be convinced of it. Your difficulty will be to grasp the degree in which truth and falsity were irrelevant in the minds of both tormentors and tormented, in discussing the question whether they should "confess" or not. You can see this fact for yourself, if you will read Krivitsky's account of the "investigation" of Mrachkovsky—the sole account yet published of the actual scene in a Bolshevik torment chamber. In ninety hours of argument with this prisoner, the questioner seems never once to have thought of trying to refute his statement that he was not guilty. Even Krivitsky seems never to have thought of it. That is not what the argument was about. It was about whether the Party under Stalin was the sole remaining hope of the revolution. If that could be established, then the lie demanded by the Party must be told. The same state of mind became apparent in the public testimony of some of the victims. They were far more eager to explain why they confessed than why they committed the crimes confessed to. And in doing so they talked for once like Bolsheviks. They justified their confessions as acts of loyalty to the revolution in a manner quite impossible to one whose acts had already betrayed the revolution.

The mystery of the Moscow confessions is insoluble only to those who do not realize what can happen to idealists who renounce the old mortal code of truthfulness, and adopt a principled belief in public lying. Although camouflaged in Russia by the intellectual verbiage of the Hegelian-Marxian dialectic, this is really the same renunciation of intelligence for animal will, of reason for blind instinct, of civilized enlightenment for barbarian "dynamism," that we see in Germany. Peter F. Drucker, in his brilliant book, *The End of Economic Man*, has described the result as he observed it among the Nazis:

"The Nazi leaders themselves never pretended to speak the truth. Beginning with Hitler's frank admission in his book that lying is necessary, Nazi leaders have prided themselves publicly on their disregard for truth and on the impossibility of their promises—foremost among them Dr. Goebbels. Not once but several times have I heard him say in mass meetings when the people cheered a particularly choice lie: 'Of course you understand all this is just propaganda'; and the masses only cheered louder. The same thing happened in Austria; the same thing in Czechoslovakia."

Anybody who understands that can understand the Moscow confessions. And he can understand why the prodigious lies told in those confessions have prospered among the devotees of Stalinism throughout the world. The question of their truth, in knife-edge form, was never raised. They were judged by the will only, the will to solidarity and power. Their function was the destruction of "Trotskyism," which is now nothing but a name for any rift, or threat of a rift, in that totalitarian will. Compared with this supreme function, the question of their correspondence with fact is subordinate altogether. To slur the question is a matter of gang loyalty.

The understanding of this mental and social process, and the clean rejection of it by a majority of mankind, is necessary to the survival of civilization. The Moscow trials, the most flagrant example of it, are therefore in some sense a touchstone of men—or at least of workingmen and liberals. Those who swallowed the lies told in these trials, or agreed to assist with silence or suspended judgment in their propagation, are to be guarded against as potential totalitarians. Those who denounced them roundly will probably defend truth, justice, freedom, scientific enlightenment.*

* Some of the earlier parts of this chapter were published at the time of the trials in the New York *World-Telegram*.

3

STALIN BEATS HITLER TWENTY WAYS

WHEN historians look back, I believe the fading of religious faith in this era will seem a chief explanatory factor of its madness. Men haven't got used yet to the emptiness of the sky, and so they worship gods of clay again—what crude and bloody ones!—and believe in myths and promises of heaven on earth. Soviet Russia was far enough away, and sufficiently insulated by the language barrier, to function wonderfully in the place of Kingdom Come. All you had to do was dismiss all the plain facts as atrocity stories—they are horrible enough to sound like it—and believe the whole state-owned propaganda, and you could be as tranquil amid the falling ruins of civilization as an infant in the arms of Jesus.

This state of religious felicity was so widespread among American liberals, and their piety is so profound, that even the Stalin-Hitler pact and the raining of hellfire on Finland have barely waked them from their pious dream. They are wistful now—it is after all a sad world—but they still cling to the belief that somewhere in the background angels hover over Stalin.

The fact is that the bombing of Finland, although it obtrudes so uncomfortably into our real world, is a polite and civilized gesture compared to the sustained content of Stalin's domestic policies. The pact with Hitler is very much easier to defend, especially for a Marxian, than the regime that Stalin is linking with Hitler's. Instead of being better, Stalinism is worse than fascism—more ruthless, barbarous, unjust, immoral, antidemocratic, unredeemed by any hope or scruple.

There is too much dispute over the connotation of fascism for one simple formula to hold. We can as yet only point to all those traits which are common to the regimes in Italy and Germany, and not to be found in even the most caste-ridden of democratic countries. I have counted twenty-two such traits, and I find that in all but two, the regime of Stalin equals or exceeds them. I wish the reader who still feels a devout anguish over Stalin as a saint betrayed to temporary sin would go over this list with me, and see if Stalin is not better to be described as a super-fascist.

(I hope that this list may also help to check a current witless tendency to apply the word "fascism" to changes made *within* the legal, moral, cultural and political framework of civilized society, whether feudal or democratic. That is playing with words, and playing on the edge of an abyss.)

1. Nationalistic emotion is hysterically exalted.

"Patriotism is the supreme law of life," was the way Stalin's *Pravda* expressed it in 1934, and he was then still hampered by relics of the old slogan of Marx and Lenin: "Workers have no fatherland." By now patriotism in Moscow must be pretty nearly the whole law of life.

2. A single party, disciplined, centrally controlled and having a monopoly of the political field, takes over the power of the state. The state is reduced to the position of a false front, whose function is to "ratify" the decisions of the party.

Needless to argue that this system exists in Russia, since it was there that Hitler and Mussolini learned it.

3. Dissenting opinion is coerced by means of patronage and intimidation to the point where the party and its leaders can assert themselves to *be* the nation as a totality. The regime is called totalitarian exactly because it is not so, but this is a threat, not a boast. It means that all disagreement or even indifference, where it cannot be bridled, will be ruthlessly stamped out.

In Russia they talk of the "monolithic party" instead of the "totalitarian state," but this only because the system is so perfect that the state can be ignored.

4. The religion of nationalism comes into conflict

with supernatural religion. The church, like the state, is permitted to exist, but its priests, and even its God, must recognize the superior authority of the party.

Under "Socialism in One Country"—which is emotionally, even more than logically, the same thing as "National Socialism"—not only religion, but *philosophy* is regimented by the party!

5. The new religion finds its focus of devotion in "the Leader," who becomes to all intents and purposes a God.

In Russia, less civilized to begin with, this return to primitive superstition has gone farther than in Italy and Germany. In many minds it has gone to the point of literal deification. The adulation of the *"Liubimii Vozhd,"* printed almost weekly in full-page headlines in the great metropolitan newspapers of Russia—"Our Beloved," "Our Infallible," "Our Incomparable Stalin," "Our Sensitive Stalin," "Our Teacher," "Our Father of Nations," "Our Sun," "Our Soul"—would provoke laughter in any Western metropolis.

6. Anti-intellectualism, in a degree heretofore found only among guttersnipes, becomes a public policy. It takes the form of flattery to the ignorant and lazy-minded, persecution, jail, death, or exile to those who stand for strenuous and honest thought.

Because of Stalin's personal jealousy of the brainier lieutenants of Lenin, and because the prejudice so easily aroused against highbrows was useful to him in overwhelming them, this policy has been more deliberately put through in Russia than in Italy or Germany. Moreover, with one exception, Stalin has not exiled his highbrows, but locked them up or shot them.

7. Anti-intellectualism also takes the form of a physical destruction of books and records, a rewriting of history and revamping of science to make it fit the momentary needs of politics.

Hitler made a public bonfire, but what Stalin has done in his craftier way to Russian books and documents and films, and even spoken memories—to all recorded truth—makes Hitler's bonfire look like an Independence Day celebration.

8. Anti-intellectualism also takes the form of an attack on "pure science"—described by the Editors of the *New Republic* as "one of the weirdest aspects of the weird Nazi ideology."

Exactly the same attack on pure science was made, with Marxian flourishes and police assistance, by Stalin's Politburo.

9. The manipulation of public opinion is substituted for its enlightenment. Human minds are regarded as receptacles for officially decreed opinions. It becomes the function of the press and radio to put over the Leader's ideas, and misrepresent those of his enemies. Debate is abolished, dogma enthroned. Whatever intellectual life

survives consists of inferences from temporary pronunciamentos of the Leader.

Here Stalin beats Hitler because he is operating upon a more primitive people.

10. Cultural isolation of the country is essential to this operation. The population is taught to believe all sorts of fables about their own merits and prosperities and the desperate condition of the outside world.

In Russia this has gone so far that private citizens cannot travel abroad, and are afraid to have friendly relations with a foreign visitor. It is, as we have seen, a crime of treason, punishable by death, to "escape across the border."

11. Party control of "scientific fact" (except in the industrial and military spheres) is accompanied by a similar control of creative art. Mussolini decrees the size of women's hips in Italian painting; Hitler suppresses as degenerate all the experimental art-works of the period.

Both Hitler and Mussolini learned this from Stalin, who inaugurated his aesthetic Inquisition in 1930. (See my *Artists in Uniform*.)

12. Immoralism takes two forms. Political lying and governmental hypocrisy are adopted as a system. Libel and slander become civic virtues. Fake plebiscites, solemn caricatures of judicial procedure, parodies of representative government, are accepted as the normal course.

"Fooling all the people all the time" becomes the essential function of the state apparatus.

Stalin's "most democratic constitution in history," with its joker guaranteeing the political monopoly of the communist party and this party's domination in every social organization in the country, is the incomparable climax of this system. It is the most insolent hoax in history. It not only fools the people all the time, but fools them with the same trick, and hands it to them hand-embossed on parchment as the fundamental law of the land.

13. Immoralism takes also the form of state-planned assassinations, frame-ups, blood-purges, Reichstag fires, piracies in the Mediterranean, etc. The worst crimes in the code of civilization become the daring virtues of the totalitarian state.

Stalin, with his deliberate starvation of four to six million peasants, his deportations of whole villages, his millions in concentration camps, his whole counties consecrated to forced labor, his execution of practically every man in the country who has occupied a prominent position within the last fifteen years, makes Hitler's little blood-purge and Mussolini's regimen of castor oil tempered with assassination, look like a sophomore hazing party. If the shed blood of innocent men were measured, Stalin's would be a lake, Hitler's a duck-pond; Mussolini's could be dipped up by the tank-carful.

14. Besides its own crimes, the state encourages the population to bait, torture and destroy some public enemy. The hate and persecution of this internal enemy serves as a peacetime substitute for war, which is necessary to keep the passion of tribal solidarity on which the whole thing is based at white heat.

What Hitler has done to the Jews compares palely with what Stalin has done to "Kulaks," and to prominent people generally. He has reversed Napoleon's maxim: "Careers are open to all men of talent." The place for men of talent in Russia, generally speaking, is the bloodstained cellar of the Lubianka prison. Still Stalin has not—as yet—overtly persecuted the Jews or other Russian national minorities. He belongs to one of them himself.

15. In baiting the Jews, Hitler revived—from the Old Testament!—the principle of tribal guilt for the crime of an individual.

Stalin has written this principle into the Criminal Code. As we have seen, his treason law holds guilty not only the family of the traitor, but everybody who lived, however innocently, in the same house with him.

16. Besides an object of hate, the tribal passion must have an object of love. There must be some real glorywork to consecrate oneself to. Accordingly, we find in all totalitarian regimes a process of economic revival or reconstruction. Absolute tyranny and complete regimen-

tation of a population does solve—temporarily, I think—one or two of the anxious problems of civilization, although at the cost of civilization itself. It is a great way of climbing out of a hole. And only in countries climbing out of a hole have such regimes been established.

Russia was in a deeper hole than Italy or Germany, and she has more abundant resources. She is a backward nation still to be industrialized. The real job to be done, the object of honest devotion, is bigger, more sure of success, more exciting.

17. The national revival is focused around and sustained by preparations for war. The war industries dominate, and the population is completely militarized from youngest childhood.

In this, Russia, Italy and Germany are alike, and Russia has now joined these other military despotisms in aggressions against peaceful neighbors.

18. Together with militarization goes a reckless campaign for increased population. Birth control is discouraged, abortions are outlawed, large families are boosted with state propaganda. Here Stalin was impeded by Lenin's extremely liberal and humanitarian legislation. He has repealed all that legislation, and Russia is now making cannon fodder with the best of them.

19. Woman is relegated to a subordinate position, and laws are passed against her independence. The total-

itarian regimes are male regimes. Woman's business in them is to breed.

Here, too, Stalin has repealed the equalitarian decrees and proclamations of the October revolution. He is traveling in the anti-feminist direction. But he is still a good way behind Hitler and Mussolini.

20. All three totalitarian governments are characterized by a paternal concern for the welfare, or at least security, of the toiling masses—in so far as they are completely submissive. This fact about fascist regimes has been little appreciated in America, but it is the foundation of their success. It is the price at which the German and Italian masses sold their freedom. In Russia, notwithstanding the legends spread by Stalin's propagandists, this concern for the toilers is no more real, and is on the whole less effective, than in Germany. The Russian masses, accustomed as they were to slavery, have sold their freedom at a lower price. In both countries all the unions are company unions, and the company is the state.

21. All totalitarian regimes make a liberal use of the phraseology of working-class revolution against capitalism. They call themselves "proletarian"; they denounce democratic nations as "capitalist"; Mussolini asserts that he is still a "revolutionary socialist"; Goebbels promises a "socialism of nations"; Hitler calls his party "National Socialist," denounces the "Jewish capitalist world";

Goering describes Germany as a "workers' and peasants' state."

Stalin uses this language more plausibly than the others, because he stems from a revolution that did involve a rising of the workers and peasants. In so far, however, as it implies that the workers and peasants run the government or receive a slice of the profits of industry, the language is as false in Russia as in Germany and Italy. The profits are disposed of by the new holders of totalitarian power, the class of bureaucrats, whose principal public expenditure is on militarizing the country mind and body.

22. In all totalitarian regimes, industry, commerce and agriculture are controlled by the state—that is, the party and its leader. "Almost the only freedom left to the German employer," says Geoffrey Crowther, Editor of the *London Economist,* "is to put his name on the firm's stationery." And Stephen Raushenbush * adds that the German "business-owner," as well as the "home-owner," shows a "perfect obedience" to the state because he knows that "it is perfectly possible for the state to take the last feature of the older system away from him."

In Russia this state control is more neat and absolute, because private claims have been abolished altogether. Control extends to the point of ownership. No one doubts that in this matter Stalin stands at the extreme

* *The March of Fascism,* 1939.

toward which the fascist states have traveled. It is indeed this very difference which seems so vast and beneficent—and so "economic"—to our semi-Marxian intellectuals that they forgive Stalin all his massacres. They think that he has built a "socialist state," and they dismiss a death-toll similar to that of the First World War with the remark that "You can't make an omelette without breaking eggs."

If we look at this difference, however, from the standpoint of either an astute capitalist or a real socialist, we find it neither vast nor beneficent, and rather more legal than economic. Raushenbush tells us that in Germany dividends are usually limited to 6 or 8 per cent, that taxes on these run up to 55 per cent, and that another 25 per cent is taken away in the form of "voluntary contributions." It seems clear from this that the employer's profits have not fared a great deal better than his freedoms under National Socialism. "The government felt no need," Raushenbush says, "for the legal evidences of ownership. . . . An essential part of its doctrine is to keep the form of private property while divesting it of almost all of the qualities formerly attached to it." And according to the French *Yellow Book* of December 21, 1939, an intimate of Hitler said: "Besides, are the Nazi and Soviet regimes so different? Aren't they almost identical in the economic field, even though with us there is a place for a certain amount of private enterprise?"

That is how the difference looks from the standpoint of capitalism. Let us glance at it from the standpoint of real socialism. The socialist program, in the days before it was taken over by semi-Marxian liberals, was, in brief: nationalization of the instruments of production and abolition therewith of the wage system of exploiting labor. Socialists of the original type had no passion for state ownership as such, nor any objection to the exchange of goods in a free market. They loved freedom more than they loved a well-organized economy. They wanted to "emancipate the workers and therewith all mankind." Nobody who cared about freedom would abolish free trade except for the purpose of achieving a more universal freedom. Nobody who hated the exploitation of labor through the wage system would take it out of the hands of private capitalists, who did it in a rather amateurish fashion, and turn it over intact to a military bureaucratic state which could do it fifty times as ruthlessly. That is what Stalin has done. He has abolished the free market, which is the progressive thing about capitalism, but preserved the exploitation of labor through the wage system, which is the regrettable thing.

I shall say more on these subjects. Suffice it to state here the bare fact, easily verifiable in detail, that for labor as for capital there is less freedom as well as less income in Russia than in Germany. In this, as in all other vital respects, except only anti-feminism and anti-

Semitism, Stalin is a super-fascist. Until the liberal and leftward democratic forces get that right, their strategy will be false throughout. At home and abroad they will be found serving the cause they profess to despise. The enemy of democracy and civilization is not any country, but the totalitarian state of mind. And that state of mind is being most successfully introduced into the United States by the adherents and fellow-travelers of Stalin.

4

THE DEATH AGONY OF AN IDEA: AN OUTLINE OF THE COMINTERN

FROM 1918 to 1921 my editorials in the *Liberator* supported all the policies of Lenin and the Russian Bolsheviks, so far as I understood them, without exception. The issue of July 1919 greeted the formation of the Third International and defended its manifesto in eight pages of almost rapturous argumentation. An editorial in May 1921, however, when I first became aware that the International had been organized in such a way as to give covert control to the Russian communist party, expressed a strenuous objection.* I could not understand this nationalistic maneuver, either from the standpoint of Marxian principle or of political good

---

* "It is to be hoped that the delegates to the next international congress will not be in such a hurry to enunciate the true principles that they can not take the pains to adopt a candid and definite and practical form of organization—an organization that will be international as well as revolutionary. . . . It will be no more possible to unite the revolutionary proletarians of all nations in an organization dominated by Russians, than it was for the Russians to carry the revolution into Poland."

sense. It shocked those very instincts which had won me to Lenin as to no other revolutionist in history.

Thus when I went to Moscow in 1922, I took with me, packed up with many enthusiasms, this troubled doubt. I hoped to find some rational answer to it, some attitude of mind, or form of procedure, among the Bolsheviks, that would reassure me as to the internationalism of the Communist International. I found, on the contrary, that this organizational maneuver had but mildly expressed their national revolutionary group-egotism.

William Z. Foster was the chief American delegate during a part of my stay in Moscow, and one day Zinoviev, the president of the International, handed him a letter ostensibly addressed to the members of the American party by its executive committee, outlining the policies to be pursued. There was a space at the bottom for Foster's signature as head of the American party, but the letter had been composed by the Russian leaders in private session. It was translated into bad English and ready for Foster's signature when he first saw it.

I had admired Foster as a real leader of the working class, a man of independent force and judgment. I expressed to him my astonishment that statesmen like Lenin and Trotsky should imagine they could build revolutionary movements in other countries under leaders whom they treated like school-boys when they came to Moscow.

"They ought to know," I said, "what a struggle for state power is, and what kind of men must lead it."

We were alone on a street-corner, and Foster, who had been a reader of the *Liberator* and always talked frankly with me about labor tactics, said:

"Max, there's a lot of things happen here that I don't like, but we've got to take it, for the present. They have the prestige, and you can't build a revolutionary movement against them."

Having taken it for the present in 1922, Foster kept on taking it for the next sixteen years, and he is still taking it. From being a strong, honest and earnestly thoughtful leader of American labor, he has become a kept messenger boy, peddling political lies and ineptitudes manufactured for the American working class by Moscow bureaucrats with half his brains and native force of character.

A day or two after my talk with Foster, Trotsky took me to visit the prison in which he had stayed when on his way to Siberia in early youth. As we drove through the streets of Moscow, I raised this question which so much disturbed me, telling him my opinion of Foster and relating the manner in which this document had been handed to him to sign.

"You know what it means to lead a revolution," I said.

"How can you imagine that revolutions in other countries are going to be led by the kind of men who will let Zinoviev—or you, or Lenin, or anybody else—write their opinions for them? You can't treat grown-up men that way, least of all revolutionists."

Trotsky's answer was:

"Well, we treat them in general, according to what they deserve. If they're grown up, we treat them that way."

"You don't get my point," I said. "No man capable of leading a revolution is going to let you decide how he is to be treated."

Trotsky was not interested. "You'll see the Pugachevsky Tower in just a minute," he said.

In that he was not different from the other Russian Bolsheviks. Although preaching a doctrine of internationalism, they were psychologically almost without exception egregious nationalists. Their heads were turned —that is the only way to express it—by the fact that under their leadership, even though in a backward country, a proletarian revolution had actually occurred. And in the opposite way the heads of non-Russian revolutionists were turned. They thought that the occurrence of a proletarian revolution in Russia had proved that Karl Marx was God, and the Russian Bolsheviks his prophets. In people who believed in internationalism— and did not believe in the critical historic role of eminent personalities—this attitude, on both sides, seemed incomprehensible to me.

Although thus disheartened about Trotsky, I thought that Lenin was becoming aware of the fatuous impracticality of this state of affairs just before he died. In his last speech to the International, I heard him say: "The trouble with this organization is that it is too Russian." And he added with his knowing smile: "For one thing, its reports and manifestoes are so long that nobody but a Russian would read them."

I may perhaps exaggerate the superior wisdom of Lenin, but at least I know that no other big Bolshevik could have expressed that revolutionary thought. Lenin died soon after, and the thought died with him. The Comintern was never an International in any sense of the term. It was an organ of the Russian communist party, founded by that party and controlled by it in a mood of impermeable national-revolutionary egotism. Its ineptitude thus emphasizes one of the most glaring flaws in the Marxian theory of history, its failure to explain nations or take any practical account of the importance of patriotism.

Still I do not think that is the whole reason for the unbelievably foolish history of the Comintern. Lenin was keenly aware in practice of the unsolved problem of nationalities, and might have organized a real International from the start, had it not been for his distinctly

Russian way of applying the doctrine of class struggle. Lenin inherited the essential temper and scheme of organization of the *Narodnaia Volia,* an incomparably heroic, fiercely disciplined, conspirative, and very tiny group of warrior-intellectuals, who fought tzarism with bombs in their few hands, and called themselves "The People's Will." They were a product of the disillusionment of the previous decade when reliance had been placed upon the people themselves, when "going to the people" had been thought the whole duty of the revolutionary intellectuals. Naïve as was their faith in bombs, they were sophisticated on the subject of the people. They assumed that, at least until the victory was won, the people could not be entrusted with the task of organizing their own will. Lenin abandoned the philosophy of the *Narodnaia Volia* for that of Karl Marx, substituting the proletariat for the people, but he did not abandon their sophistication. He never permitted himself to believe, as most Western Marxists did, that "going to the proletariat"—that is, enlightening their class interest—was the essential duty of the Marxian intellectual. On the contrary, he burst into the Marxian movement, somewhat like a bomb himself, with the announcement that the proletariat by itself not only could never arrive at socialism, but could never arrive even at the idea of socialism. That had to be "brought in" by the tiny minority of the intellectuals, the "cultured representatives of the possessing classes" who were imaginative enough to interest themselves in the cause of the proletariat. Lenin's book *What To Do,* which laid the foundations of the Bolshevik party, expressed this peculiarly Russian point of view so vigorously that he himself, even after the October revolution, hesitated to release it in the West. I once asked Karl Radek why it was not better known, and he told me he had often urged Lenin to let him translate it, but Lenin would only laugh and say:

"That's too stiff for those Westerners. They can't swallow it."

The story of the Comintern is, in some sense, the story of an unsuccessful attempt to make "those Westerners" swallow the doctrine that a fiercely disciplined, conspirative small group of warrior-intellectuals has a right to function as the Workers' Will.

F. Borkenau, in his *World Communism, A History of the Communist International,* a work of rare intelligence and thoughtfulness, has elaborated this fact. I think he overstresses the distance between Lenin and the Western left-wing socialists on the question of a revolution against political democracy. I myself, in the *Liberator,* defended the dissolution of the Constituent Assembly by the Bolsheviks on the basis of class dictatorship, regardless of whether it represented a majority of the nation or not. However, I knew nothing, and few

Western socialists did, about Lenin's doctrine of the Party as the will, and also intellect, of the proletariat. That certainly had to be "brought in" by cultured representatives of the *Russian* possessing classes, and its conflict, not only with Marxism as an objective belief about history, but with the instinctive feeling of the Western movement that the workers must accomplish their own emancipation, is a second reason for the mad behavior of the Comintern.

Not only were each of the constituent parties organized like Lenin's, with warlike concentration and a war psychology, but the whole International was organized in the same way. It was strictly disciplined, conspiratorial and under command from headquarters. Headquarters being in Moscow, and the Russian communist party having a preponderance in the Executive Committee, the commanding staff of the Russian party was the commanding staff of the world revolution. It was, still more fatally, the main source of its funds. The degree to which the international prestige of the Soviet revolution was enhanced by contributions from the treasury of the Soviet state, is inadequately appreciated even by those who like to play it up. In this new, Moscow-dominated machine of world-wide civil war, the "professional," or wholly consecrated, revolutionist—so nobly conceived by Lenin in Russia in the days of the unaided struggle for power—tended to become "professional" in a far less arduous sense. Indeed, apart from such matters of personnel, the tendency of the whole system was not only to dominate the revolutionary movement of the West, but in large yet subtle ways to corrupt it. And this still more repelled the native leaders of any genuine revolution in the West, and left the Comintern detached by the very method of its attachment to the European labor movement.

The divergence was of course deepened, and the disaster made complete, by the failure of the revolution led by Lenin's party to liberate the Russian proletariat. It can hardly be doubted that had any substantial part of Lenin's shining promises in his *State and Revolution,* and other writings of the revolutionary days, been fulfilled—had any gleam appeared of the substantial hope of their fulfillment—the Western movement would have accepted his brilliant system of revolutionary engineering, whether Marxian or not. "Leninism" would have spread throughout the world, and we should be well forward on that clearly posted road toward the free and classless society.

Not only did the Russian revolution fail to free the workers and peasants; it failed in such a way as to cast the first and most alarming doubt on Lenin's special innovations. The very organization led by professional revolutionists who spoke *for* the exploited masses turned out, when power was in its hands, and itself in the hands of an ordinary politician—exceptional in force and cunning only—to be the instrument of their abject enslavement. The monstrous blood-smeared misbegotten Iron Heel of a thing that emerged in the place of either a workers' republic or a return to democratic forms, could not but confirm the doubt in Western minds as to the practicality of the whole scheme. At the same time organizations directly copied after Lenin's began to be used in Italy and Germany and other Western countries with the express purpose of keeping the masses patriotic and perfecting their subjection to the state. Stalinism and fascism, the one an outgrowth, the other a by-product, of Lenin's system, form the third reason for the nightmare history of the Comintern.

C. L. R. James, whose *World Revolution* is another useful contribution to this history, still believes that "Leninism is the only solution of the problems of the modern world." "But," he adds, "there was too much need of Lenin in both the planning and the execution of Leninism." If Leninism needs Lenin, then it is not a valid procedure for creating out of the given materials of human nature a free society. For Lenins are, perhaps, of all types the least frequently given. Certainly no other extreme revolutionist in history ever possessed Lenin's moral and intellectual endowment. The swiftness with which the collapse of his plans followed upon his death, the impotence of his colleague, Trotsky, to stem the tidal reassertion of crude power-thirsty human nature, revealed, as plainly as James' passage of praise reveals, the flaw in those plans. It grew more and more obvious to thoughtful revolutionists throughout the whole twenty years of the Comintern's history.

Let us examine now the astounding contour of that history.

CRAZY ZIGZAGS

The Communist International, founded hastily and almost without foreign delegates in 1919, took its first important action at the second congress in July 1920. The action was to split the world's labor and socialist movements with an ultra-revolutionary platform-ultimatum of twenty-one points. These twenty-one points, based on the assumption that the world was in a state of "acute civil war," outlined an assault not only against capitalism and the capitalist governments, whether politically democratic or not, but against all socialists who believed in political democracy. They demanded that all Western revolutionists accept the Bolshevik organizational system and the disciplinary leadership of the Russian Bolshevik party (points 12 and 16). It seemed almost as though this organization, offering leadership to a mass movement deemed to be in actual progress, was directing at least half its fire, not against the enemy, but against these democratic socialists whom it considered the false leaders of the movement. If they refused to sign on the dotted line beneath the whole twenty-one points of militant class war, they were denounced as "social patriots." A communist Trade Union International was formed at the same time and labor unions which refused to join it were described as "yellow." A feeling went abroad, backed by the prestige of the Russian revolution, that not only political principles or interpretations of Marxism were at stake, but courage, manhood and sincerity in the struggle for an economic, or proletarian, or *real* democracy.

Finding itself isolated by these extreme tactics, not only from the democratic socialists, but from the working class itself, the Comintern made a sharp rightward turn in 1921. It adopted the slogan "To the masses," and rapidly developed this into the policy of the "United Front" with yellow and social-patriotic organizations. The idea was to join these organizations in a struggle for certain specific ends, and by showing superior zeal in the struggle to win the workers away in general from the Social Patriots. It was a matter of "showing up" the yellow leaders as really loyal to the bosses, and of no value to the working class. In practice, of course, the showing-up was done as much by whispering campaigns as by superior zeal, and the communists thus appeared to normal minds to be not only zealous, but also treacherous. They would promise loyal co-operation with an organization when their real purpose was to destroy it. The Western workers, lacking the mystic revolutionary absolutism of the Russians, found it hard to understand this divorce of socialist standards from those of ordinary honorable conduct. Largely for that reason the United Front policy proved more successful in breaking down the "leftism" of the communists than in winning the workers away from the right-wing leaders. By 1922 the Comintern had so far abandoned its twenty-one points as to sanction, in certain circumstances, participation in the yellow "labor governments." And by 1923, it was itself ready to put down and kill with "yellow" policies a genuinely revolutionary rising of the German workers.

Except for Russia in 1917, there has never been, I suppose, in the world's history a more perfect set-up for the seizure of power by a proletarian party than in Germany in 1923. Not only were millions of the workers and peasants consciously waiting for it, but they were waiting for the existing communist party to perform it. To defend itself against this revolutionary party backed by millions, the tottering government had, thanks to the Versailles Treaty, only a hundred thousand soldiers. Lenin was now out of the picture, and Trotsky, too, pushed aside, and it was probably Stalin's letter to Zinoviev and Bukharin—"In my opinion the Germans must be curbed and not pushed on"—which finally killed the

German revolution. Still the general policy of the Comintern at that time was a rightward one. Whatever Lenin might have done—or Trotsky, if he had been in a position to insist effectively upon action in Germany—the fact remains that the International organized by him and in accordance with his system as the spearhead of a world revolution, failed miserably at this first real test.

It failed not only miserably, but ridiculously. Brandler, designated from Moscow to be leader of *the* German Revolution, when he saw *a* German revolution actually rising round him, could think of nothing more leaderlike to do than run to Moscow for "instructions." That is pitiable enough, but let us read what happened to this "leader" after he arrived in that remote place. I quote from C. L. R. James:

> "For days he went from office to office, but the leaders of the world revolution evaded him and he could not get an interview. At last, at the very end of September, he had a meeting at which Stalin and Zinoviev were present. They gave him the extraordinary instruction to enter the Social Democratic Government in Saxony and form a Workers' Government. Brandler refused. He knew that to do that would be the death of the revolution. They told him that the entry was for the purpose of arming the proletariat and so preparing for the insurrection. He replied that if this was the aim, before the entry there should be intensive preparation both in Saxony and the rest of Germany. Without that, the entry into a Social Democratic Government would be a sign of

a retreat, and not of preparation for revolution. Stalin insisted on immediate entry, and under the Bolshevik tradition of discipline which Stalin knew so well how to abuse, Brandler gave way, making, as he has since confessed, the greatest mistake of his life. But Stalin (as always working secretly) was taking no chances. Against Brandler's wishes, Zinoviev, as President of the Executive Committee, sent a telegram to the Communist headquarters in Saxony ordering them to enter the Government at once. To ensure that Brandler would not take any individual action, he himself was instructed to enter the Government also. Every avenue of escape was blocked."

We need not harrow ourselves with further details of this caricature of revolutionary leadership. Suffice it to note that less than three years after its promulgation of the famous twenty-one points of ultra-revolutionism, the Comintern employed its organized authority and the prestige of the Russian revolution to "curb" the one entirely auspicious and unqualified insurrectionary movement of an industrial proletariat that has occurred in modern history.

As soon as the crisis had passed, however, and all hope of action by the masses was destroyed, the Comintern took another sharp turn, and passed to a *more extreme* leftward position than that of 1921. Brandler was detained in Moscow—blamed of course for the "failure" of the German revolution—and his adventurist opponents, Ruth Fischer and Maslow, were put at the head of the German party, and a manifesto issued: "The task of arming the workers and of technically preparing for a decisive struggle must be carried on with tenacity."

I mention Germany because Germany was central at the moment, but it is one of the peculiar and most dreamlike features of the Comintern that its meaningless sharp turns in policy have been, almost without exception, applied simultaneously, and regardless of local conditions, on a world scale. Under the influence of this second extreme swing to the left, which lasted about two years, ultra-revolutionism and anti-democratic bigotry prevailed everywhere. The Bulgarian party, which held the balance of power in the country, stood aside while Stambouliski's Peasants' Government—the most progressive thing in postwar Europe—was overthrown by a military dictator. The party was too "revolutionary" to care whether the peasants or the military were in power. At this time also (December 1924) Zinoviev sent a small gang of Russian adventurers into Esthonia to organize a *Putsch*. The full account of this episode as given by Borkenau is well worth reading, but Mr. James sketches it adequately, with its general background, in the following paragraph:

"For nearly a year Communist Parties all over the world, working on this directive, compromised themselves before the workers, and by their adventurism and needless violence weakened themselves and strengthened the growth of the Social Democracy. The most tragic expression of this exaggeration came in Esthonia where at 5:15 A.M. on December 1, 1924, 227 Communists started a revolution, and by 9 o'clock were completely defeated, doing untold harm to their own party and the idea of proletarian revolution all over the world."

Six months later (April 1925), a group of Bulgarian communists attempted to destroy the military government, for whose existence they were responsible, by blowing up the Sofia cathedral while all its ministers, together with the king, were attending service. They killed scores of people and died themselves, but missed the government. This unsuccessful adventure was frowned on in Moscow—or more accurately, repented of—but throughout this period anybody who was not ready for extreme action of the same general kind was proscribed as a traitor to the working class. In many countries the democratic socialists, now renamed "Third Party of the Bourgeoisie," replaced the capitalists as the main object of attack.

Toward the end of 1924, all this ultra-revolutionism began to be abandoned. In 1925 another world-wide rightward swing occurred, and this again was *more extreme* than that of 1922-23. The Bolsheviks of the Red Trade Union International were soon sitting with the British trade union leaders, the most "yellow" in the world outside the United States, in the famous Anglo-Russian Committee. Here they sanctioned with the prestige of the Russian revolution the liquidation of the

British general strike of 1926. At this same time the American party tried to affiliate with the Farmer-Labor party of the La Follettes. The Polish party gave a left-handed help to the seizure of power by the military dictator Pilsudski. And in China, in the name of the "Long View," every principle of Lenin, every pretense of dynamic belief in the class power of workers or peasants, was thrown over. The formation of soviets was forbidden. The Chinese revolutionists were literally disarmed by the Comintern, and betrayed into the hands of Chiang Kai-shek to be massacred.

Again let us pass over the harrowing details. Suffice it to know that once again in the history of the Comintern a spontaneous revolutionary mass movement occurred; once again it was damped down and snuffed out by this fabulous organization.

And once again, incredible as it may seem, as soon as the betrayal was complete, the crisis past, and all hope of action by the masses safely dead, a new extreme left turn was made. Not only were soviets and arms and insurrection called for in China, but in general, beginning in the summer of 1927, a new "Third Period" of "acute civil war" throughout the world was proclaimed from the turrets of the Kremlin. And here again the limits reached in the previous left swing were far surpassed. For almost six years the Comintern represented everything that Lenin had warned against as "the infantile disease of leftism in communism." Every kind of cooperation with democratic socialists and reformist organizations was absolutely banned. Whole staffs of officials, in some cases whole memberships, were expelled from the constituent parties. The "Social Patriots," or "Third Party of the Bourgeoisie," were given the still fouler name of "Social Fascists." They were proscribed and vilified in almost unbelievable language, and not proscribed only, but physically assaulted, and their meetings broken up by gangs of thugs. The essential animus of this "Third Period" was directed, not against capitalism at all, but against democratism as represented by the social democratic parties. The thesis was promulgated that, as between social democrats and fascists, the fascists were the lesser evil. In the spring of 1931 the German communist party, acting on orders from Moscow, actually joined Hitler's Nazis in a campaign to overthrow a Prussian government in which the democratic socialists held a dominant position.

In 1933, when Hitler came to power, the communists not only failed to raise a fist against him, but greeted his advent as a step forward toward the workers' revolution. They continued to denounce the democratic socialists as traitors to the working class after their party had been dissolved by Hitler. They accused them, while they were in concentration camps, of devising "new knavish forms of collaboration with the bourgeoisie."

Even when a few months later, in heroic contrast to themselves, the Austrian socialists took arms against a reactionary dictator, these communist denunciations did not cease. The head of the Czechoslovak party wrote:

"The parties of the Second International try to make capital out of the blood of the Austrian proletariat, try to cover with its blood their interminable betrayals and crimes. But the facts convict these hyenas and traitors, the facts prove incontestably that the Austrian Socialist Party has brought the proletariat under the knife of Fascism."

Borkenau, who quotes this passage, asks the very natural question: "What was the good of the whole international split, if the communists did not fight and the socialists did?" But the question is more serious than that. The communists not only failed to fight against the reaction; they fought with it. In that same month of February 1934, when the Austrian socialists were dying on the barricades for democracy, the French communists joined the extreme right-wing reactionaries in an armed march on the Chamber of Deputies, attempting to overthrow the government of the radical party, and not unwilling, if it fell out that way, to overthrow the republic.

That was the extreme point of the leftward spasm which began in 1928. The march on the Chamber of Deputies occurred on February 6, 1934. On February

12, the French communists issued with the "yellow" trade union leaders a joint call for a general strike—an act of collaboration with "hyenas and traitors," which rapidly led the way to a complete abandonment, not only of the hysterical anti-democratism which had led them into Hitler's camp, but of all proletarian revolutionary aims, principles and intentions whatsoever. It was not a "united front" with democratic socialists now. It was a "Popular Front" with all who believed in any way, shape or manner in "democracy"—a renunciation of the basic doctrine of class struggle and the whole Marxian view of society and history. This reached its insane climax in Stalin's statement to Roy Howard that the Bolsheviks had never wanted a world revolution at all, that the whole thing had been a "tragi-comic misunderstanding."

Under the Popular Front slogan the Comintern wormed its way into the governmental and educational and publicity institutions of the democratic countries to such an extent as to become a mighty power. And then once more—for the third time in its history—a genuine revolutionary movement occurred within its field of operation. The masses of the Spanish workers and peasants rose in arms, not only against a dictator, but against the capitalist state. And now the Comintern was not content to join the social democrats in putting down a revolution. It went far beyond them—so far as to attack them from the right—in its enthusiasm for the maintenance of "democracy" in Spain.

This period of ultra-rightism—which in America included voting for Roosevelt and defending the New Deal against its *socialist* critics—lasted from 1934 to 1939. In the autumn of 1939, the communist fatherland made its pact with the Nazi fatherland, and the slogan of democracy was again abandoned by the Comintern. With Earl Browder's announcement in September of a "quick transition to socialism," Americans were informed of the beginning of a new reign of "leftism," a Fourth Period, in which (outside Germany) the Comintern will function once more, if it survives, as an instrument of violent world revolution.

I have purposely refrained from mentioning, except for Lenin's death, any specific cause of these successive "rightward" and "leftward" leaps, or twitches, of the Comintern. The fact that the organization, while posing as international, was really controlled from Moscow, is a most obvious cause, so far as the leadership is concerned. The exigencies of Russian foreign policy, or the reverberation of factional fights in Moscow, can be traced in most of these sudden shifts of policy. But the fact that the organization could survive them, the somnambulistic behavior of the rank-and-file, has also to be explained. I doubt if any other organization in history ever went through a similar process. I have drawn a pic-

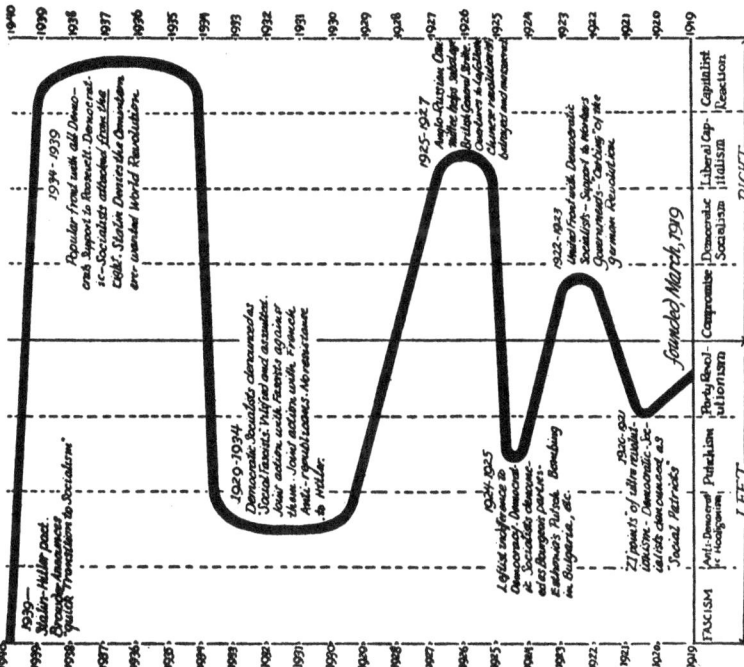

ture of it on the preceding page, and as you see, with each spasm the arc traveled, no matter in which direction, becomes more and more extreme, until finally, first on one side and then on the other, all principles are thrown off, all trace of the original creed and motive of its being. It repudiates the workers' revolution on the extreme leftward swing by joining with the fascists, on the extreme rightward swing by joining with the anti-Marxian democrats.

In this condensed form the history of the Comintern looks like the death-shudder of an expiring idea. And that, I think, in a deep sense, is what it is. The idea was that a higher democracy could be arrived at by an antidemocratic revolutionary procedure. It was, as we have seen, a Russian idea, created by grafting the organizational principles of the *Narodnaia Volia* upon the Marxian scheme of progress through working-class struggle. The Marxian philosophy was, to be sure, of such a nature as to make the grafting possible, and I do not think the Russianness of the idea, or even the control from Moscow, was the essence of the trouble. The essence was that people who believed in democracy, and wanted to make it more perfect, undertook to do so by destroying what democracy there was and denying every democratic instinct in themselves.

The meaning of "left" and "right" in such a situation is not simple. "Left" means readiness for extreme anti-democratic action in loyalty to a higher conception of democracy. "Right" means readiness to compromise the higher conception and cling to what democracy there is. As faith in the possibility of achieving a higher democracy through anti-democratic action grew weaker with the failure of the experiment in Russia, a process of oscillation between the existing democracy and the anti-democratic procedure was natural. Natural, too, that the oscillations should grow more and more extreme. Natural that the final swing should shake off all those deeply loyal to democracy, and carry to the tyrants' camp those infatuated with the anti-democratic procedure.

5

TROTSKY'S DIVORCE OF ENDS AND MEANS

IN THE first half of his life Trotsky voiced the very criticism of Lenin's organizational system which is now on the lips of all socialists anxious about the real future of humanity and the working class. He described Lenin's idea of the Party as the sovereign vanguard of the class as "the replacement of the dictatorship of the proletariat by a dictatorship over the proletariat, of the political rule of the class by organizational rule over the class." And of Lenin's intra-party regime called democratic centralism he said with true foresight: ". . . The apparatus of the party substitutes itself for the party, the Central Committee substitutes itself for the apparatus, and finally the dictator substitutes himself for the Central Committee."

Trotsky surrendered to Lenin on this organizational question in 1917, as the actual revolution approached. On the political question, however—his perspective of a "permanent" revolution as against Lenin's of a "democratic dictatorship of the workers and peasants"—Lenin surrendered to him. If he had the breadth and flexibility, and the self-reliance—for that is his deep lack—to declare that he has proven right and Lenin wrong *on both counts,* he could offer real leadership in the present crisis. He could, incidentally, improve the picture of his whole life as it will look in history.

But Trotsky is too much concerned with proving—what is least of all in need of proof—that he is a revolutionist. Stalin's trick of dragging up these old differences and representing him as "bourgeois" and "anti-Bolshevik," has exaggerated this concern. He is becoming steadily more and more shrill and rigid in defending the extreme organizational dogmas of Bolshevism. He seems, indeed, in a recent article,* to have set his teeth in a determination to out-Lenin Lenin.

He dismisses the problem of workers' democracy, the relation of the vanguard party to the class, with a finality that seems to me foreign to Lenin's mode of thought. Answering one who finds the error of the Bolsheviks in excessive centralism, mistrust of ideological struggle, mistrust of the masses, lack of the freedom-loving spirit, he says:

"Only a party wielding the authority it has won, is capable of overcoming the vacillation of the masses

* "Moralists and Sycophants Against Marxism," the *New International,* August 1938.

themselves. To invest the mass with traits of sanctity and to reduce one's program to amorphous 'democracy,' is to dissolve oneself in the class as it is, to turn from a vanguard into a rearguard, and by this very thing, to renounce revolutionary tasks. On the other hand, if the dictatorship of the proletariat means anything at all, then it means that the vanguard of the class is armed with the resources of the state in order to repel dangers, *including those emanating from backward layers of the proletariat itself*. All this is elementary; all this has been demonstrated by the experience of Russia. . . ." [My italics.]

The "experience of Russia" is, of course, exactly what suggests to judicious minds that something must be the matter with "all this." I cannot help thinking that had Lenin lived to see how easily his party of the vanguard was turned into a party of the rearguard of the workers, and thence—still "wielding the authority it has won"— into the party of a new and counter-revolutionary class of bureaucrats, he would have had new things to say about the manner of determining its relation to the working class. Lenin had an underlying fluent human wisdom, a sense of the concrete relations between social ends and means, which was deeper than his programmatic ideas, and, in a manner of speaking, contained them. He would not have ignored the close historic and practical connection between his scheme and that of the fascists. He would have realized that in the present world this question of the self-appointed vanguard party as against the democratic sovereignty of the class is posed anew. He would have wanted to do something about it, or think of something to do in the future.

In his Testament, where Lenin notified his party that Trotsky was "the most able" of its leaders, he also warned them against Trotsky's disposition to be "carried away by the administrative aspect of things." He might have added "by the logical relations of ideas." For with all his brilliant fluidity and mastery of concrete detail, Trotsky is inclined to schematic thinking. He often seems to be living more in his head than in the human world.

Perhaps in so far as democracy of class is concerned Trotsky has merely expressed Lenin's views in a more extreme and absolute form. When he proceeds from that, however, to the question of *democracy within the party,* and reduces this from an organizational principle to a question of programmatic expediency, I think he has transgressed, not only the intuitive wisdom of Lenin, but his actual principles. I quote from the same article:

> "The internal democracy of a revolutionary party is not a goal in itself. It must be supplemented and bounded by centralism. For a Marxist the question has always been: democracy for what? for which program? The framework of the program is at the same time the framework of democracy."

Centralism, being an abstract noun, cannot, of course, supplement or bound anything. The Central Committee can, but since the Central Committee is elected by the membership after free discussion, it also cannot supplement or bound democracy. The Central Committee, if honestly elected, *is* democracy functioning as best it can in a party engaged in complex, and at times conspiratorial, affairs. "Centralism," then, as something which can supplement and bound democracy to fit the framework of a program determined by itself, can mean nothing but the boss or bosses, the Politburo, the Secretariat, the Leader and his gang. I do not see what other meaning can possibly inhere in Trotsky's words.

Applied specifically, this would mean that in his famous fight against Stalin in 1923 and after, Trotsky was defending intra-party democracy, not because he believed in it *as* a program, but because he believed the rank-and-file as then inclined would support the program he advanced. The framework of democracy, if extended at least to the bottom layers of the party, happened to coincide with the framework of his program. Or, in plain United States, the party if they had a chance to vote would vote for him. Had that not been so, he would, according to this doctrine, have been justified in replacing Stalin's "centralism" with his own.

I have in the last fifteen years so often defended Trotsky against this assertion on the part of his enemies, that I find myself tempted to defend him against himself.* But I can see no way to do it. He seems to me, in this statement about intra-party democracy—"The question has always been: democracy for what? for which program?"—to have cast loose from all moorings, not only in Marxism and in Lenin's writings, but in intellectual honesty and good sense. "Democracy for what? for which program?" is a contradiction in terms. It is using terms for the purpose of moral and intellectual confusion. It is the democracy of Hitler's plebiscites, of Stalin's constitution.

We learned from Marx that in the cause of socialism popular democracy must be abandoned for the dictatorship of the proletariat. We learned from Lenin that proletarian dictatorship must be abandoned for the dictatorship of the Party. We now learn from Trotsky that party dictatorship must be abandoned for the dictatorship of the Center. It is but one step, and the step inevitable, to the *Fuehrerprinzip*. Aside from the sincere belief of the existing Leader that he dwells in an upward-

---

* Owing to my defense of Trotsky's position and translation of his works, it is commonly assumed that I have been "an ardent Trotskyist." Trotsky and I never had any misunderstanding about this. Our conversation and correspondence have been peppered with sharp encounters about my Marxian heresies and their consequences, and Trotsky has steadily threatened to devote an appendix in his *Life of Lenin* to my theoretic annihilation. I suppose I am now saving him the trouble. He will dismiss me, in the light of this book, by "administrative decree."

going universe, and one which has revealed to his mind the road by which it is in process of producing a superdemocratic society, and his personal consecration to that goal, I fail to find in this system of concentric departures from democracy any guarantee whatever that the interests of the proletariat, to say nothing of mankind at large, will be ultimately defended. I fail to find any dynamic and real differentium between this new philosophy of "Democracy for what? for which program?" and that of Hitler and Stalin.

As though to repel the last thoughtful friend he had, Trotsky concludes his article with a cry for "ruthlessness" on the part of the "proletariat" (reduced to this minute Center of an unelected vanguard) and a proclamation of immoralism that is a proletarian paraphrase of Dr. Funk and Goebbels:

"To accomplish the overturn the proletariat needs all its strength, all its resolution, all its audacity, passion and ruthlessness. Above all it must be free from the fictions of religion, 'democracy' and transcendental morality—the spiritual chains forged by the enemy to tame and enslave it. Only that which prepares the complete and final overthrow of imperialist bestiality is moral, and nothing else. The welfare of the revolution—that is the supreme law!"

It seems to me that anybody cherishing the ideal of a free, humane and democratic society who would, in the present state of the world, sign up to such a set of propositions, is more reckless than revolutionary, more mad than Marxist.

Let us read for relief an outline of the kind of society Trotsky imagines he can arrive at by this anti-democratic and immoralistic overthrow:

"In a society which will have thrown off the pinching and stultifying worry about daily bread, in which community restaurants will prepare good, wholesome and tasteful food for all to choose, in which communal laundries will wash clean everyone's linen, in which children, all the children, will be well fed and strong and gay, and in which they will absorb the fundamental elements of science and art as they absorb albumen and air and the warmth of the sun, in a society in which electricity and the radio will not be the crafts they are today, but will come from inexhaustible sources of superpower at the call of a central button, in which there will be no 'useless mouths,' in which the liberated egotism of man—a mighty force!—will be directed wholly towards the understanding, the transformation and betterment of the universe—in such a society the dynamic development of culture will be incomparable with anything that went on in the past." *

Was there ever a more dangerous divorce of ends from means?

* From *Literature and Revolution* by L. Trotsky.

6

THE MOTIVE-PATTERNS OF SOCIALISM

IN THE old days of faith and propaganda, socialism seemed a wonderful idea because it offered to solve so many problems at once. It would put an end to wage-slavery and make all men genuinely free and equal. By substituting co-operation for competition, it would also make human solidarity real; even the Christian ideal of universal brotherhood, and of losing oneself in order to find it in the common good, would cease to be merely a theme for Sabbath-day sermons. It would also relieve us of the "anarchy" of capitalist production, and make possible a planned and scientific efficiency in the important business of keeping alive. And then, almost incidentally, it would put an end to wars, which are, you see, just a by-product of this unfree-and-unequal unbrotherly-united, unplanned and inefficient way of doing things.

Because it offered to solve all these various problems, socialism appealed to people with widely differing patterns of volition. Without pretending to be exhaustive, we can divide them into three main groups: first, the rebels against tyranny and oppression, in whose motivation the concept of human freedom formed the axis; second, those yearning with a mixture of religious mysticism and animal gregariousness for human solidarity—the united-brotherhood pattern; third, those anxious about efficiency and intelligent organization—a cerebral anxiety capable of rising in times of crisis to a veritable passion for a plan. The anti-war motive entered, with differing colors, into all three patterns. And each of them usually contained as a subordinate factor the motive that was central in the other two.

This versatility of socialism that seemed so wonderful in the days of ideal propaganda is the principal cause, I think, of the confusion prevailing among socialists now that they are confronted with results. The Marxian promise was that all three patterns would attain their "closure" when the dictatorship of the proletariat had expropriated the private capitalists, and society as a whole began to conduct the business of production. Stalin's regime of totalitarian state ownership frustrates the central motive of the first pattern, shatters it completely. To libertarian socialists, therefore, no matter how "monolithic" it may become, nor how much industrial planning and solving of unemployment problems it may do, Stalin's Russia is a counter-revolutionary state.

To the gregarian or human-solidarity socialists, on the other hand, the Soviet Union, notwithstanding prison camps and the massacre of dissenters—notwithstanding the perfected exploitation of the workers—is now, as never under Lenin's restive leadership, the promised land.

To those primarily concerned about businesslike organization, while not perhaps a promised, Russia seems at least a promising land. Particularly to the disillusioned liberals, brought over to socialist ideas by the crisis in capitalism and yearning above all things for a plan, a "solution of the economic problem," an island of order in the mounting waves of change, Stalin's Russia has a master fascination. It carries to an extreme that very putting away of childish things like Justice and the Rights of Man and going in for realistic hard sense about economics, with which they themselves are trying to fill the forlorn spaces in their hearts. Although the repressed forces upon which it rests are ominous, and its regimentation of opinion bodes ill even for the Planning Commission, the "socialist fatherland" is at least to be apologized for in other lands—certainly not denounced from the standpoint of a mad dream like "emancipation of the workers and therewith all mankind."

THE LIBERTARIAN MOTIVE

In those who built the Marxian movement, and those who organized its victory in Russia, that act of emancipation was the central motive. They were, as some are prone now to forget, extreme rebels against oppression. Lenin will perhaps stand out, when the commotion about his ideas subsides, as the greatest rebel in history. His major passion was to set men free. Ignazio Silone has expressed the opinion that "in every Marxist worker the strongest basis for his socialist faith is the sentiment of justice." But that is perhaps mainly a different way of naming the same passion. It is hard to separate freedom from equality, equality from justice, as a social aim. Equality of rights and privileges is justice, and if any are free, it is just that all should be. Nevertheless, if a single concept must be chosen to summarize the goal of the class struggle as defined in Marxian writings, and especially the writings of Lenin, *human freedom* is the name for it. Time and again during the spring and summer of 1917, in speeches and articles tense with excitement and carrying the whole weight of his personality, Lenin reiterated this essential aim and purpose of his actions:

"Do not allow the police to be re-established;
"Do not allow the re-establishment of the all-powerful officialdom which is in reality not subject to recall and belongs to the class of landowners and capitalists;

"Do not allow the re-establishment of a standing army separated from the people, serving as a perpetual incentive for various attempts to crush liberty and to revive the monarchy.

"Teach the people, down to its lowest strata, the art of administration, not through books but through actual practice to be begun immediately and everywhere, through the utilisation of the experience of the masses.

"Democracy from below, democracy without an officialdom, without police, without a standing army; discharge of social duty by a *militia* comprising a universally armed people—this will insure the kind of freedom which no tsars, no pompous generals, no capitalists can take away."

In his deliberated program-pamphlet, published on the eve of the seizure of power, the same motive is only more studiously spoken:

"Only in Communist Society, when the resistance of the capitalists has finally been broken, when the capitalists have disappeared, when there are no longer any classes . . . *only then* 'does the State disappear *and one can speak of freedom.*' Only then will be possible and will be realized a really full democracy, a democracy without any exceptions. And only then will democracy itself begin to wither away in virtue of the simple fact that, freed from capitalist slavery, from the innumerable horrors, savagery, absurdities and infamies of capitalist exploitation, people will gradually *become accustomed* to the observation of the elementary rules of social life, known for centuries, repeated for thousands of years in all sermons. They will become accustomed to their observance without force, without constraint, without subjection, without the *special apparatus* for compulsion which is called the State."

MOTIVE-PATTERNS   133

These sayings reveal the central motive in most proletarian revolutionists who come from the "educated classes." And the feeling in the proletarians themselves who become consciously revolutionary, although at times more filled with hatred for the oppressor, is not often very different. It is in both cases a fighting passion, and the thing fought for is liberation. The thought that by expropriating the oppressors a victorious proletariat can remove the "absurdities" of capitalist production and introduce an orderly economy, is incidental. It is not a reason for the change, but a guarantee that it will be permanent, seeing that it satisfies good sense as well as revolutionary passion. The fraternal-solidarity idea, too, is spectral in the revolutionary's mind. He has no real distaste for competition, as his neglect of the co-operatives, except as auxiliaries in the class war, plainly shows. Even his hatred of international war is not pacifist. It is a hatred more of military regimentation than of fighting. The *standing army* is what Lenin fulminates against. That is his pacifism. He wants the whole population armed! And why? Because it will "insure the kind of freedom which no tsars, no pompous generals, no capitalists can take away."

Lenin was a man of intense personal reserve, but after his death, at a memorial meeting of the Moscow soviet in the Great Opera House, his widow spoke frankly about his motives:

"Comrades, during these days that I have stood by the body of Vladimir Ilych I have been thinking his whole life over, and this is what I want to say to you. His heart beat with a burning love for all the toilers, all the oppressed. He never said this himself—no, and I should not say it at a less solemn moment. I speak of it because he inherited this feeling from our heroic Russian revolutionary movement. This feeling is what impelled him to seek fervently, passionately for an answer to the question: 'What is to be the path of liberation for the toilers?' "

THE UNITED-BROTHERHOOD MOTIVE

Lenin did not find the path of liberation for the toilers. He led them with the red flag flying down the road to a more dreadful tyranny than he or they had dreamed of. He died, saddened by the first intimations of this tragedy, and with a warning against the tyrant on his lips. All his close disciples, all those imbued with his deep passion for human freedom, have been killed as irreconcilable enemies by the tyrant.

It is a part of our confusion, however, that some of them died equivocal deaths. Some of them died confessing that they, not Stalin, were the traitors to the new socialist society. Their confessions were irrelevant to truth, but such confessions could not have been forced from such men had they not been bewildered about the truth. Like so many socialists elsewhere, they could not quite make up their minds whether Stalinism is the counter-revolution or not. Their philosophy had taught them that a confiscation of private capital would lead with historic necessity to the free society, even though it had to pass through an apparently opposite regime; perhaps it was still on the way. That was one source of their confusion. But their philosophy had also taught them to expect other things besides freedom in that ideal society, a new kind of human solidarity, a mystic state of things in which all arts and activities would become "collective"—and therewith a planned economy and an end of international war. Russia was anti-war, and was planning her economy, and was—albeit with the help of firing squads and the GPU—manifesting a supernal solidarity. Maybe they *were* after all unconscious traitors, John the Baptists who could not recognize the coming of what they themselves had prophesied. Maybe their concern for freedom was too impatient. Maybe it was excessive. Maybe it was selfish.

Something like this passed in the hearts of those old Bolsheviks who died uttering the confessions of treachery dictated to them by Stalin. In their socialism the freedom motive was probably less central than in those who died behind closed doors, crying, "Long live the workers' revolution!"

It is certain, in general, that this motive has proven less organic, less universal, than was anticipated by those champions of emancipation who laid the foundations of socialism. And the unity or solidarity motive has proven more organic, more universal. It has proven strong enough to permit in the name of socialist brotherhood those same deeds of blood and torture which made Christian brotherhood at times a curse to Europe. It seems as though, whenever people talk of all mankind as brothers, it is Cain and Abel they are thinking of. At any rate, it proves surprisingly easy for those dominated by this seemingly so large and amiable ideal to satisfy it within a narrow, bigoted and cruel group. They make their group coterminous with humanity by treating as non-human all those who will not join it. This seems a contemptible and dreadful trick, but it is undoubtedly accomplished in many cases with sincere idealism.

So many yes-men and clamoring lickspittles flock around as soon as power is won, that it is then difficult to distinguish the sincere idealists of brotherhood, but they are always present. There is no hypocrisy, for instance, in Michael Gold's devotion to Stalin's totalitarianism. Misrepresenting Stalin's enemies is one way of expressing his devotion, but in the devotion itself there is no lie. All through life this Jew without Money had been seeking for submersion in a Totality, seeking to lose himself in the bosom of a substitute for God. A similar thing, I happen to know, is true of Michael Kalinin, who has discovered such amazing survival-value in the storms that swept down Lenin's following. It is true of Harry F. Ward, whose testimony before the Dies Committee regarding the League for Peace and Democracy, of which he is Chairman, was so shocking to those acquainted with the facts. This Christian minister too, as his book, *The Profit Motive,* shows, is actuated by the thirst for co-operative emotion, for the sense of membership in a totality. It is that organic passion which leads him not only to excuse the lies and crimes of totalitarianism in Russia, but himself to participate in a totalitarian attempt against public enlightenment in the United States. Stalin himself in his unctious moments describes socialism as a "fellowship" rather than a free society.

Undoubtedly this fraternal passion—for that, unhappily, must be the name of it—formed a part of the original motive-pattern of socialism. And the fact that it finds satisfaction in the totalitarian state-capitalism of Stalin, where human freedom is a dead idea, is a principal cause of the interminable confusion, the no man's land, the welter of divided minds and split libidos, bequeathed to us by the Russian revolution in the place of a world socialist movement.

THE PLANNED ECONOMY MOTIVE

Another element of confusion is introduced by those bourgeois liberals and Fabians who have taken up the job of apologizing for Stalin out of an anxious interest in orderly and planned economy. Four or five years ago in the *New Republic,* Edmund Wilson made the suggestion that the liberals should "take communism away from the communists." * It seemed at the time almost a nonsensical remark, but it is exactly what the liberals (minus Edmund Wilson) have done. Despairing of the old faith in democracy and education, and shocked by the crisis of capitalism into a sense of their own futility, they have, on the whole with surprising explicitness, adopted not only the program of socialization, but the name and, in a manner peculiar to themselves, the general philosophy of Marxism. Since they executed this maneuver in a kind of flight from the old principles of liberalism, it is natural that Marx's extremer concept of liberty should have small place in the pattern of their socialism. They are definitely not interested in the emancipation of the working class. The brotherly-union concept is somewhat less alien to them because it is a part of the respectable tradition of Christianity. But the focal thing in their mind and motivation, when they make bold to call themselves socialists and even appeal to the authority of Karl Marx, is his extreme solution of the economic problem. For the sake of that, they are prepared to forego, or kid themselves about, everything else that they ever believed in. In this way it has happened

* Quoted from memory.

that the "strongholds of American liberalism," the *Nation* and the *New Republic*, became our chief apologists for the most unliberal, unprincipled and bigoted and bloody tyranny in modern history. They became "socialist." So great and so confusing is the variety of motives appealed to by the too opulent concept of socialism.

TOTALITARIAN LIBERALS

To my mind these neo-Marxian ex-liberals are at present a greater menace than the Stalinists to the cause of freedom in America. Their intellectual hunger for the solution of a problem brings them into a position similar to that of the despairing masses driven by a more urgent hunger. They have not only apologized for totalitarianism in Russia, but they have helped to camouflage its propaganda-stratagems and pressure-plots in this country. By abandoning their faith in popular intelligence, in open and complete debate, by lending their pages to the manipulation as well as the enlightenment of public opinion, condoning political immoralism, adopting an attitude of *Realpolitik* wherever such antique concepts as the Rights of Man are in question, and in general outdoing Marx in being hard-boiled on all questions except that of proletarian power, they are, while professing themselves its friends, giving aid and comfort to the enemies of democracy. They are doing exactly what the same groups did in Germany before 1933—breaking the faith in the republic of those who should be its firm defenders, destroying the mental and social habits which make democratic institutions successful, easing us into the Totalitarian State of Mind.*

A typical illustration, indeed a perfect epitome of this, is George Soule's little volume called *The Future of Liberty,* but which should be called *Preface to an American Totalitarianism.* Mr. Soule begins his book by expressing his fervent affection for the words to be found in our Declaration of Independence and Bill of Rights. He has, he tells us, "an ineradicable confidence that somehow or other such words are valid; that they provide, if properly defined and applied, an indispensable frame of reference and standard of value." Taking "liberty" as the nuclear word in these documents, he demonstrates his newly acquired "Marxism" by explaining that the groups who first employed it, and most of those who have employed it since, were not expressing a love of freedom for mankind at large, but were seeking a free field for their own special interests. At this point his Marxism recedes, and instead of going on to show that the freedom fought for by the working

---

* At the time of the second Moscow treason trial I wrote a letter to the *Nation* which its Editors declined to publish either in whole or in part. Although too dated, and perhaps too full of the moment's indignation, to have a place among these mature reflections, it seems to me to deserve publication, and I have placed it in an appendix to this volume.

class must in the nature of the case be freedom for everybody, he imagines a suspension of all special interests, and takes up the problem of the future of liberty under state ownership, no matter how it might be introduced or who might own the state.

Although remote from Marxism in its original form, this is a real problem, and one very much needing to be solved. A downright effort to solve it would begin, it seems obvious, by recognizing that liberty means absence of governmental restraint, and would proceed to inquire whether, within what spheres, and to what extent, people who might be described as sane and not criminal could enjoy this blessing under a system of industry owned, planned and controlled by government. It would then further inquire by what means their enjoyment of such liberty could be established and guaranteed.

Instead of solving, or even confronting, this hard problem, Mr. Soule eludes it by the simple process of "redefining" liberty. And the process is simple indeed, for it consists of calling liberty the exact opposite of what it is. Liberty, Mr. Soule informs us, is to mean "subordination"! This astounding announcement, which would probably not stand up on a page of type by itself, is made plausible by adding "to a common purpose," a phrase which fits in well enough with Christian lore and tribal instincts to lull our logic to sleep.

After enlarging for many pages upon the values to be achieved by transferring the name of liberty to a condition of subordination to common purpose *as such*, or *any* common purpose, Mr. Soule lets it out almost incidentally—although just at the moment when our logical faculties were beginning to revive—that the common purpose he has in mind is not war, glory, territory, or any of those common purposes with which history has made us so familiar. It is "an equitably shared abundance." This again sounds noble, almost as noble as the Declaration of Independence, and again lulls us into imagining that something has been said about The Future of Liberty.*

That Mr. Soule is really preparing the ideological path for an American totalitarianism is evident in his bland ignoring of the question *how this new and quite unusual purpose is to be made "common,"* and the still more obvious question—to one objectively concerned about liberty—*what is to be done with those who fail to fall in with it, or who have dissenting views about how it is to be achieved?* On these objective questions what Mr. Soule is really saying, I hope unconsciously, is that

---

* These remarks about George Soule's book were first published in the *Yale Law Review*. My comment there concluded as follows: "Since we can not attain all the ideals of the Declaration of Independence, let us guard as our most precious heritage its mental temper. If we have to surrender our liberties in the cause of organization, let us say so. If we have to surrender a part of them, let us say what part, and how many. Let us confront our problems with a clear and downright mind."

MOTIVE-PATTERNS 143

people who will not fall in line are going to be jailed, shot, sandbagged, herded into concentration camps, or otherwise put out of the way, but that instead of being done in the name of *Subordination* to a Totalitarian State or Monolithic Party, this is going to be done in the name of *Liberty,* the Bill of Rights and the Declaration of Independence—redefined.

Mr. Soule's book concludes, quite naturally, in a word of praise for the totalitarian regime set up in Russia on the ruins of the dream of Lenin, and rationalized into the beginnings of a millennium by similar "redefinitions" of the language of the revolutionary fathers—and by shooting the fathers. Even the deliberate swindle of the masses perpetrated by Stalin in his "democratic" constitution Mr. Soule finds courage to describe as a significant aspiration. Why is Stalin's phony constitution a "significant aspiration," while Hitler's phony plebiscites are a travesty of popular government, they both being in fact foul cheats and insults to civilization?

The reason is that in the motive-pattern of Mr. Soule's socialism, the focal thing is a solution of the economic problem. Surrounding this, and like a Christian halo sanctifying it, is the sentiment of surrender to a social whole. Only in the outer fringe there lingers, wistfully, a ritual affection for the phraseology of freedom. To put *more* meaning, an economic as well as a political meaning, into that phraseology of the "bourgeois" revolution, was the central motive of Marx, and certainly of Lenin. Mr. Soule's reading of Marx impels him to take all the real meaning out. But this is not a trick. It is not a crass process of betrayal. It is an instinctive shift of elements in the too opulent pattern of socialist motivation.

LIBERTARIAN RADICALS

The sole way out of the confusion is to distinguish the three patterns, and make more discriminating declarations of allegiance. There can be no truce between libertarian socialists and those whom the fraternal or gregarious impulse renders tolerant of totalitarianism. This does not mean that human freedom as a political concept excludes a moral attitude, or even an evangel, of universal friendliness. The wish to extend free life to all mankind is not an unfriendly wish. But those who want to see men really free, each to enjoy the values of his own life in his own fashion, will have to abandon the religion of the collective will. They will have to decide whether by socialism they mean individualism generalized and made accessible to all, or whether they mean a general surrender to some authoritative concept of the collective good.

For my part, I have not the glimmer of a desire to lose my identity in a collection, nor would I wish this loss upon a single workingman. The essential meaning of the revolution to me was the liberation of individuality, the extension of my privilege of individuality to the masses of mankind. I endorse absolutely the words of Lenin, published just before the revolution: "The more initiative, variety, daring, creativeness are brought into play by the masses, the better"; and the words of Trotsky published shortly after: "The revolution is, first of all, an awakening of human personality in those masses heretofore assumed to be without it."

To those sharing these aims, and yet lacking the faith of Lenin and Trotsky in a benign evolution of the very forces of production, the solution of the economic problem has also, of course, an absolute importance. We cannot move toward this more real and universal freedom—nor even perhaps preserve the freedoms that we have—unless we find out how to distribute goods and still continue to produce them. Marx was wholly right in declaring that men must first keep alive, before they can occupy themselves with higher values. But that is very far from subordinating freedom to efficiency, or postponing it, or reducing it to a spoken ritual. Those who take this line, and bless it with a little thought of brotherhood, are also marching, however little conscious of it, toward the totalitarian state.

Here again the terms "right" and "left" have lost their simple meaning. The question is whether you are seeking primarily, and at any cost, a solution of the economic problem, or whether you are seeking a solution which will preserve the liberties that came with capitalism and foster their extension in the future. Between these two positions, as between the totalitarian and the libertarian, there can be no truce. There can be no truce between a civilized community and a herd stampeded into an up-to-date corral. The concept of human freedom, with its corollaries, justice and equality, forms the axis of the motive-pattern of all who can be called radicals.

PART TWO

Socialism Reconsidered

7

THE PREDICAMENT OF THE WORD "SOCIALISM"

STALINISM, as we have seen, contains all the evils of Nazism or Fascism, most of them in extremer form. But there is one vital and complete difference. Fascism, notwithstanding verbal bluff and bluster, has no doctrine. It has no civilized ideal. Fascism is a sheer drive for power, a naked exaltation of the tribal passion of fighting solidarity and submission to the chief. It is "action for action's sake," "organization for organization's sake," * criminal gang-rule as the chief end of man—an obviously suicidal renunciation of civilized values.

Stalinism is not obviously suicidal. Stalin's renunciation of civilized values justifies itself by an appeal to Marxian theory. His gang-rule clothes itself in socialist ideals. He preaches a super-civilization, and presents his tyranny as the beginning of it. Since his regime differs

* The phrases are borrowed, one from Peter F. Drucker's *The End of Economic Man*, the other from Herman Rauschning's *The Revolution of Nihilism*—two indispensable books to those who wish to understand Hitler's Germany.

from Hitler's principally in being more savage, this makes it far more dangerous to the outside world. Only people in despair take up with naked gang-rule. But gang-rule dressed as the classless society, the workingman's republic, the *success* of the Russian revolution, the beginnings of real freedom and equality, appeals also to hope. It appeals to uncritical intelligence. It is spreading throughout the whole world—the healthy and liberal as well as the diseased and despairing parts of it—the virus of totalitarianism. It is teaching free and social-minded people the habit of voluntary irrationality and intolerance—an intolerance relaxed completely toward a single party and its leader, who have free scope of criminality and hypocrisy in the grab for power.

The success of the Stalinists in this enterprise of corruption is helped vastly by a cloudiness in the popular meaning of the word "socialism." The old socialist programs had declared that democracy, to be real, must be economic, and that to make democracy economic, the working class, acting through the state, must take over the land and instruments of production, and replace the wage system of class exploitation by a system of free cooperation. For propaganda purposes this was generally shortened down to *socialization*—or *nationalization—of the means of production*. To uncritical minds the dominant ideas conveyed were that real social changes are economic, and that state ownership of the land and industries is, or will produce, real democracy, real liberty and equality, real human culture.

Under Stalin the industries have actually been nationalized, and the major part of the land taken into collective ownership. And this basic change—momentous indeed to have happen in one's own lifetime—quite naturally seems to uncritical minds to *be* socialism. It seems, at the very least, to be that alteration in the "economic substructure" which they have learned is the proper scientific or "Marxian" foundation for it. When they are further assured that the new regime is actually working, that human beings still eat and sleep and laugh and smile in Russia, and that the state has wealth and armed power and speaks with authority among the nations, they feel that the millennium has begun. Or more accurately, they feel that any socialist who does not endorse this new regime, and explain away all its crimes as missteps and incidental evils, is himself "looking for a millennium." He is not scientific, not Marxian, not a practical realist. All practical realists, and especially those trained in Marxism, will subordinate every other issue to the defense of the Soviet Union.

Critical minds, trained by actually reading Marx, are able to point out that so long as exploitation through the wage system survives, and the state which has taken over the industries is in the control of a single monolithic party, the industries are not really nationalized—

much less socialized. The change is not socialist—or in so far as it is socialist, it is not economic, but merely legal. It is a magniloquent writing of "social ownership" on paper, the very kind of ideological delusion against which Marx, with his passionate insistence on economic realities and the realities of class power, was in revolt. The party leaders who control the state control the income from the state-run industries, and thus form the axis of a new ruling class. This new ruling class exploits the workers by the same technique as the old—that is, by paying wages which do not equal the value of the work done. And they exploit them, as a simple matter of fact, with more, rather than less, irresponsible ruthlessness. In so far, therefore, as socialism means a more real democracy, a society without class exploitation, a "society of the free and equal," to use Marx's own phrase, there is not only no socialism in Russia, but no beginning of it—no step that actually leads, or can lead, toward it.

Power has been taken from the workers, and the wage system has not been touched. It cannot be touched now except through a forcible expropriation of the new bureaucratic class or gang. Such expropriation seems, and may indeed be, more difficult than the expropriation of a disorganized and anarchistic class of private capitalists. If that is so, then Russia is farther from real socialism, not nearer to it, than the bourgeois countries. In any case Russia is off on a by-road, and her government is no longer in any respect a guide or leader of the socialist movement. That much is clear to all critical minds who care about the original aims of socialism and understand its theories.

But the difficulty does not end there. The Stalin bureaucrats are not merely the betrayers of a successful revolution led by genuine Marxians; they are its outcome. Stalin's totalitarianism is not only a parasitic growth upon a nationalized industry; it is an inherent part of the process of nationalization in the only case in which it has been tried. Where it has been half-way tried—where only the control of industry has been nationalized—as in Germany and Italy, a similar, although less extreme, reversion to criminal or savage tribal life-forms has been entailed. The presumption is a natural one that totalitarian gang-rule belongs intrinsically to this process of nationalization. And the more one studies the workings of human nature, both in individuals and in classes, in Russia, Italy and Germany, the more probable does this presumption seem. Far from being an offhand impression, it is the impression left after a mature and varied exercise of judgment. And it puts the thinking socialist in a very weak position.

He has to fight the vulgarizers of his doctrine, the dupes of the Stalin propaganda, who assert that Stalinism, merely because it has "nationalized" the means of production, *is* socialism, in the sense of being a classless society. But all the time he suspects in the depth of his mind that, in a more tragic sense than they realize, the vulgarizers are right: Stalinism *is* socialism, in the sense of being an inevitable, although unforeseen, political and cultural accompaniment of that nationalization and collectivization which he had relied on as part of his plan for producing a genuine classless society. If he is still thoughtful, still critical, still honest with himself, he can hardly help inwardly doubting, at least, lest this be true. There was never anything in his doctrine but an inheritance of Christian optimism to prove the contrary. And that doubt, both in his mind and in the public's, makes him an unconvincing adversary of the satisfied totalitarians, who assert that Stalinism *is* thoroughgoing socialism and he a bourgeois renegade who, when it came to the real thing, would not go through.

From this predicament the socialist loyal to the aim of a more real democracy could save himself only by introducing into his own program some scheme designed to *prevent* nationalization from entailing totalitarian regimentation. It is not a new idea to him that these two might be found inseparable. The socialist program itself but little antedates the "old and oft-repeated objection that Socialism means 'barracks for the masses,' 'bureaucratic rigidity in ruling the masses.'" I quote from Lenin, who dismissed this old objection on the

THE WORD "SOCIALISM" 155

eve of the October revolution with the glowing promise of "that type of republic where, from top to bottom, there is no police, no standing army, no officialdom enjoying the privileges of irremovability, . . . public service through a really universally armed people's militia, composed of men and women, a militia capable of replacing the bureaucrats—all this combined with election and instant recall of all public officers, and with payment for their labor according to proletarian standards."

Lenin promised this type of republic as "the practical business to be launched without delay." The non-fulfillment of his promise was a blow to socialism from which it cannot recover by making new promises exactly like the old. A new promise, however, is all that any of the anti-Stalin socialists have made. Those surrounding Trotsky accept the basic principles of totalitarian gang-rule, the one-party tyranny and immoralism in the cause of power, but promise that in a sufficiently advanced country, and provided the gang has the right leaders and a genuine proletarian policy, there will still emerge, even though like a rabbit out of a hat, the society of the free and equal. The democratic socialists are more plausible, but they too only assure us that they are not going to let it happen again. They are going to "learn from the failures of post-war Germany and Russia, and make social ownership go hand in hand with increasing democratic controls." * So long as they do not state exactly what they have learned and how they are going to "make" this happen, the suspicion is inevitable that when it comes to an issue, they will sacrifice either democratic controls or the actual expropriation of the capitalists (and most probably the latter). In either case, as leaders toward a society of the free and equal based on state ownership, they remain, notwithstanding their better morals and more persuasive manners, as unconvincing as the Trotskyists.

Neither of these remnant groups is facing the real question raised by the assertion of the Stalinists that the totalitarian tyranny which has emerged from the socialist triumph of October 1917, and the subsequent campaigns of nationalization and collectivization, *is* socialism.

In these circumstances, it seems likely enough, and not improper, that language itself, or the intuitive wisdom of the race, will decide that the Stalinists are right. It will decide, I mean, that the totalitarian state is the political form natural to a collectivized economy, and that the name for this phenomenon is socialism. The dream about the abolition of the wage system and the return to the worker of the surplus value of his toil—the real aim of socialism to those who founded it and

* Quoted from *Keep America Out of War* by Norman Thomas and Bertram D. Wolfe.

THE WORD "SOCIALISM" 157

organized its victory—will be filed away along with internationalism as a part of the literary *Weltanschauung,* the social myth by which the great totalitarian national consolidation was achieved.

This etymological outcome, which seemed probable to me while I was writing this book, has been made more probable by the Stalin-Hitler pact. The world is finding out that that pact is no temporary maneuver, but a vital union of two profoundly similar regimes. Whether the effect of their union will be to carry the German fascist revolution clear through to state ownership, as Herr Rauschning has predicted it will go, whether under German influence Russia will relax the foreign trade monopoly and grow more lenient to private enterprise, or whether these two trends will meet in some middle ground, depends too much upon the issue of the war to be foretold. I suspect that the capitalists and landlords in Germany will suffer under Stalin's influence, and perhaps even be swept away, but that under Hitler's influence the new Russian ruling class, the bureaucrats, will be strengthened in their hold on privilege. Dr. Ley, the head of the German Labor Front, was permitted to issue a proclamation concluding: "Socialism against capitalism! That is our battle cry!" (November 18, 1939.) Here the influence of Stalinism is apparent—especially since Dr. Ley's real business was to announce an extension of the labor day from eight to ten hours without additional pay. On the other hand, *Pravda* announced (almost on the same day) the reopening of twelve private markets in Moscow!

However that may go, the propaganda union of Stalinism with Nazism, the alliance of the Swastika with the Hammer and Sickle, in a world-wide propaganda for "socialist" revolution, can—unless the war says no—be confidently expected. The official staffs of the various communist parties will accept this new directive, and take up the new task, with hardly a break in their ranks. The American *Führer* will announce to the same faithful "twenty-two thousand" in Madison Square Garden, with the same insolent solemnity with which he has announced every other abandonment of principle dictated from Moscow, that the October revolution was one way of moving toward socialism, the maneuvered shift of power in Germany in 1933 another.

There is no resilience in mere names which will enable "socialism" to resist this combination of great powers. Words have no loyalty. It is by changing their meanings that popular intelligence, although incapable of new definitions, remains flexible and elastic. Even to me, the proposal of Clement R. Atlee, leader of the labor opposition in Parliament, that England adopt socialism as a means of winning the war, sounded hollow and unreal. It sounded almost like a joke. England is fight-

THE WORD "SOCIALISM"

ing two totalitarian states both calling themselves socialist, and to win the fight is sacrificing a large block of those liberties which distinguish her from these states. If, besides organizing the war, she undertook to organize a nationalized industry and agriculture, is there any doubt that she would sacrifice the rest? Where is the guarantee that British Military Socialism would be any better than German National Socialism or Russian Socialism in One Country? Where, in general, lies the guarantee that government-owned or government-controlled industry does not as its natural political form beget the totalitarian state? In my opinion it is this question, half-unconsciously and blindly asked by the masses, which has undermined the prestige of authentic socialism, and so weakened the American party that it cannot hold its place on the New York State ballot. When National Socialism joined hands with Socialism in One Country over the grave of Polish independence, the word "socialism" became, to say the least, a liability to any genuine movement of liberation.

In my present opinion it became not only a liability, but a misnomer. For I think the tendency of the language is probably right. I think that the democratic socialists and the Trotskyists have failed to suggest any scheme by which total governmental ownership of industry can be dissociated from totalitarian government because there is none. I think that when we fully confront the worse than negative result of the Russian experiment, and assume our intellectual responsibility, which is to think out a scheme of distribution for an economy of abundance *not* involving totalitarianism, we shall find our scheme different enough from the old socialism to require a different name.

It is, at any rate, our responsibility and our duty to do this thinking.

8

SOCIALISM AS PHILOSOPHY OR SCIENCE

THE failure of the Russian revolution is perhaps the greatest tragedy in human history, terrible in the breadth of its impact, terrible in the depth of its significance, terrible in its personal details. Other revolutionary martyrs have been permitted a heroic death; the heroes of the Russian revolution have been shot like dogs in the cellar. If this tragedy, when at last it is faced by loyal and thoughtful men, is not to throw them back into cynicism or despair, it must be faced as the unhappy result of a legitimate experiment. To cry "Socialism is dead! Long live socialism!" may satisfy a momentary impulse, but will not long sustain a thinking will. When an experiment fails, intelligence demands that we re-examine the theories upon which it was conducted, and rectify them in the light of the result. The whole result of the Russian development is of course not yet in sight, but plenty is in sight to show that it will have little in common with the aims of socialists, whether utopian or scientific. Plenty is in sight to warrant a re-examination of the principles from which it set out.*

Trotsky, the ablest exponent of the theory and natural critic of the experiment, declines to take this step. In *The Revolution Betrayed* he raises the question of "radically revising our traditional views of the socialist society," but only to decide against it. Asserting that the prodigious success of the Soviet Union in increasing production has demonstrated the "practicability of socialist methods," he blames its equally prodigious failure to show the beginnings of freedom and equality upon "lack of the means of subsistence resulting from the low productivity of labor" in a backward country. That and the "tardiness" of the revolution in more advanced countries are for him adequate explanations of the whole disaster. And he has drawn the vigorous moral: "All those for whom the word socialism is not a hollow sound but the content of their moral life—forward!"

Socialism is not the content of my moral life. I have always regarded socialism as an effort to solve a specific problem and one only of the engrossing problems that confront our human nature. And this perhaps embold-

* This chapter and the next were written before the two preceding. They were published as an article, "Russia and the Socialist Ideal," in *Harper's Magazine* for March 1938. It may prosper my thoughts in the reader's mind if he remembers that. In particular, I have not tried to weave into these chapters the psychological analysis of socialist motivation undertaken in Chapter 6.

ens me to perceive a little more adequately than Trotsky does the scope and significance of the Russian failure. I do not believe, either, in the Marxian legend of universal "upward" evolution, which supports him in his somewhat cursory reaction to this collapse of our hopes. Moreover, I am completely detached from party struggle, and not vitally concerned about revolutionary prestige. I am in a position to regard Stalin and his dictatorship, not as an enemy, but as a result. For these reasons, although not in some ways equipped as Trotsky is for the task, I am going to suggest what seem to me the main points in that "revision of our traditional views" which he declines to make.

THE PHILOSOPHICAL BELIEF

I have spoken of the Russian revolution as an experiment. But it was not an experiment to those believers in the Marxian philosophy who stood at the head of it. To them it was a step in a general process of whose "historic necessity" they were convinced in advance. Only its details were experimental. A great many of their miscalculations were due to this fact, so many that we must begin our revision of the socialist theory by removing from it this element of philosophical belief. We must restate the theory in the form of hypothesis, before we can revise it with a free mind in the light of experiment.

Marx inherited his philosophical belief from Hegel.

It is a belief that the world is evolving of its own necessary motion, and by a "dialectic" procedure, "from the lower to the higher." He attributed this kind of evolution to a world which he called, in opposition to Hegel, "material." But he did not, and could not, define the word "higher" merely in a material sense. He meant by "higher" more ideal.* And the ideal he had in mind, so far as concerns human society, was that of the utopian socialists. It is the simple conception of men living together reasonably, generously and justly, without class exploitation, without war, and with freedom for everybody and a fair chance to grow. Such a state of affairs is approximated in any good-natured and happily situated family, and that is why it seems so natural a hope for humanity at large. The Christian evangel and the doctrine of "natural rights" have made it seem still more axiomatic to many minds, but I think Thomas More indicated the deep source of the socialist ideal when he proposed, in his *Utopia,* to draw the picture of a whole nation that lived "like a single family."

Marx assumed, on no other basis but a turning other-side-up of Hegel's philosophy, that the world about him was in process of realizing this ideal. He was studious

---

* Engels, in an exposition of their common philosophy read and endorsed by Marx, replaced the word "higher," in eulogizing the dialectic universe, by "more magnificent." "The celestial bodies, like the formations of the organisms . . . arise and perish and the courses that they run . . . take on eternally more magnificent dimensions."

both of books and of events; he was rich in ideas; he made many contributions to knowledge; but he never questioned that assumption. He never therefore really tried to prove it. The essential labor of his mind was to discover *how* a material and yet dialectic world would evolve from capitalism toward a family-like mode of social life, and to find his place and that of all serious-minded socialists in the process. And the result of his labor, to summarize it briefly and therefore inadequately, was this:

A dialectic process, according to Hegel, is a process of advance by inner conflict or self-contradiction, and the resolution of this conflict in a "higher unity." In human society this inner conflict is to be found in the economic phenomenon of class struggle. And in modern society it is to be found in the struggle, not so well-known in Marx's time, of the proletariat against the capitalists. It is this new struggle which is destined to resolve itself in the higher unity foreseen and advocated in so detached and impractical a manner by the utopian socialists. The ideas of the utopians are, indeed, only a "symptom" in the mental world of this approaching material change. The mere development of the technique of production will bring it about "with iron necessity" that the workers will seize the power, expropriate the capitalists and "socialize" the means of production. A period of proletarian dictatorship must intervene, but this dictatorship will inevitably die away as the new and higher form of social life emerges. Nobody can describe this "higher social form" in detail, but obviously it will be that "society of the free and equal" which is striven after in so soft and foolishly impractical a way by the utopian socialists.

The way to strive after it is to join the harsh struggle of the workers against the capitalists, make the struggle revolutionary, make it "conscious of its destiny," make it lead as rapidly as possible to the seizure of power, the inauguration of class dictatorship, and the beginning of the process of socialization.

That is the Marxian theory stripped of the prodigious wealth of factual and ideational material which Marx and his followers have brought under it, or built into it, or remarkably illumined by means of it. It enables the Marxians, notwithstanding the extreme humaneness of their ideal, to be hard-headed, realistic, ruthless, and even to a degree cynical, in their pursuit of the ideal. It is through clash and bloody conflict that society advances; good and evil are merely names for the two forces through whose contradiction "higher forms" are born. The only ultimate good in a world thus inevitably going upward through struggle is to be on the right side of the struggle. And the only valid knowledge is hostile criticism from the point of view of the class destined to conquer.

Marx believed that this ingenious philosophy, besides reconciling tough-minded realism with tender-minded aspirations, removed the mystical or utopian element from such aspirations. He thought that since he had attributed his ideals as end-terms to the natural evolution of a "material" world, it became perfectly sensible and scientific, and indeed a kind of super-science, to believe in them. But it is not sensible to take utopian aspirations out of your own head and attribute them to the external world. And no matter how much you disguise the process by calling the world "material," and by invoking the word "scientific," it is not science to do this. It is just the opposite—religion. It is primitive, unverified and unverifiable belief in what you want to have come true.

There exists no proof that the world is traveling of necessity and by its own motion toward something "higher" in the human sense—much less in the sense of the utopian socialists. To minds trained in experimental science the very pretense to know the "historically necessary" result of capitalist evolution, even did it not fall in so pat with the author's wishes, would have, if proposed today, the aspect of a grandiose delusion. The apparent success of the Russian revolution has given an adventitious prestige to this austere pretense at knowledge. But the failure of the revolution will rapidly destroy it. Notwithstanding his notable contributions to science, Marx's system as a whole will be set down as wish-fulfillment thinking in a form as crude and antiquated as it is ingenious. Marx will take a place in history not unlike that of Rousseau—a man behind the highest scientific attitudes of his time, but borne to great heights because he created a new *Weltanschauung,* and one which fell in with the passions, aims and tactics of a great social movement.

The *Weltanschauung* will live forever, a priceless treasure, comparable to those of Sophocles, of Dante, of Aquinas, of Spinoza. The incidental contributions to verified knowledge will also live and be acknowledged. But as a system pretending to be scientific, and indeed to be a kind of super-science, Marxism will be laid away with Thomism, Calvinism and the rest. The sole use science has for *isms* made out of a man's name is to ridicule subjective and unverified emotional beliefs. Only in a general return to medieval darkness could this romantic metaphysics—"saturated," as Trotsky well says, "with the optimism of progress"—really conquer modern minds.

We have no certain knowledge where the world is going, whether "higher" or "lower." We have no knowledge how much we, any one or all of us, by taking thought can swerve it. But we care where it is going. And it does not seem impossible that by a process of experimentation, if we hold ourselves free to learn all we can from each experiment, we may succeed in drawing up some plan for arriving at a more reasonable and decent general form of social life.

PHILOSOPHY OR SCIENCE 169

THE PRACTICAL HYPOTHESIS

What made the Marxian metaphysics so acceptable, of course, was that the *action* proposed by it seemed reasonable. Restated in the form of a working hypothesis, a plan to be tried out, Marxian socialism was as good as anything anybody in its epoch had to propose. So restated, it would read somewhat as follows:

The opinion of the utopian socialists, that men might live together in society much as they do in happy families, if land and the instruments of production were owned in common, and wealth justly distributed, is perfectly reasonable; the aim may be attained. It cannot be attained, however, by regarding present-day society as a unit and preaching to everybody the reasonableness of the idea. Society is too sharply divided into classes for that, and people in general react to ideas too much on a basis of class interest. That very fact, however, can be turned to account by those who believe in the socialist idea. Let them enter into the present-day class struggle on the side of the exploited classes. The difficulties of capitalist production are such that crises are bound to occur. As foreign markets are used up, these crises will become more and more severe and far-reaching. In some nation-wide and perhaps world-wide crisis, if a political party having socialist aims and resting essentially on the workers, has made adequate preparations, it will be possible to seize the political power by main force, expropriate the capitalists and declare the land and instruments of production the common property of all. *After* that, the processes of education and evangelism, so futile under the present class system, will become effective. Men are reasonable and malleable enough, and life will be enough happier in such a society, so that after a brief period of dictatorship by the new ruling class, co-operative relations will become established in custom and habit. No dictatorship, and in fact no public power whatever, will long be necessary. The state will quite naturally die away, and men will find themselves living together in large societies, and indeed ultimately all over the planet, in a state of equality and freedom, tolerance and mutual helpfulness.

That is the revolutionary socialist hypothesis, abridged and stripped of detail just as we stripped the Marxian dialectic theory. To persons buffaloed by intellectuality as such, it will sound more naïve, but to those who know what thinking is, it is obviously more mature. And it indicates, of course, the same general line of action:

Join the harsh struggle of the workers against the capitalists, make it revolutionary, make it conscious of its possibilities, make it lead as rapidly as possible to the seizure of power, the inauguration of class dictatorship, and the beginning of the process of socialization.

Only the substitution of *possibilities* for *destiny* differentiates the two programs. And yet in the long run the difference is deep between those who are consciously trying out a hypothesis based upon quantitative judgments and probability, and those who conceive themselves as co-operating with a process expressing the ultimate nature of the universe, and assume that their destined goal is knowable on other grounds than the experiment itself. It is as deep a difference as can separate two minds interested in the same project.

Some people think that only the religiously believing minds will be resolute enough to wage a serious struggle, but the evidence of history is against them. Struggles of this kind have been waged, and waged with great violence—notably the American revolution—with a clear sense of the hazards involved and no philosophy but naked resolution. Indeed the characteristic function of optimistic systems of belief is not to sustain action at all, but to offer consolation when it fails or seems impossible. The Mensheviks, in trying to postpone the proletarian revolution in 1917, were as much supported emotionally by their certainty of its ultimate triumph as the Bolsheviks were in speeding it on. Lenin himself, in all particular crises of action, explicitly rejected that sense of sure victory which in a more general way his philosophy gave him. "There is no such thing," he asserted, "as a situation with only one possible outcome." And in the critical days before October, he repeated in a thousand different variants the thought: "We must take the hazard of action now!"

Those who persuade themselves that in order to win a social struggle we must bandage our eyes and go in like blind bulls, are worse than historical reactionaries. They are biological defeatists. Man has no superiority over the powers of nature but his intelligence, and any proposal to set a limit to the free growth and movement of that is an attack against man, no matter how accompanied with trumpets and triumphal banners. What has to be done with blinders on had better not be done.

9

DEFECTIVE BLUE-PRINTS

ONCE the Marxian theory is restated as a working hypothesis, or in other words a simple plan of action, its chief defect becomes quite obvious. In any well-deliberated plan of action three elements can be distinguished: definition of the end to be attained, examination of the conditioning facts, and mode of procedure by which it is proposed to pass from the facts to the end. It is in the definition of the end that Marxism falls most obviously short of the standards of science, and it is of this only that the present chapter will treat.

The fact is that Marx, owing to his belief that Reality-as-such is a dialectic procedure toward something "higher," did not bother to define his end at all. He left that task to Reality-as-such.

"It is not a question," he said in early life, "of putting through some utopian system, but of taking a conscious part in the process of social transformation which is going on before our very eyes."

To those able to identify science with an optimistic philosophy, such a cavalier attitude to the crux of the problem seemed worthy to be called scientific. And the whole mid-nineteenth century was so "saturated" with optimism, that this was actually put across as scientific socialism. I have been bitterly criticized for calling Marxism a religion, and yet what is Marx actually saying in that famous sentence but this:

"The way to avoid utopian schemes is to have no schemes at all—put forth your efforts in the right direction and leave the rest to God."

And he said the same thing a quarter of a century later when commenting on the Paris Commune:

"The workers well know that in order to realize their own emancipation, and at the same time the higher form toward which the present society tends *by its own economic forces,* they will have to pass through long periods of struggle which will transform both circumstances and men. *They have no ideal to realize, they have only to set free the elements of the new society which the old bourgeois society carries in its womb."* * [Italics mine.]

Any engineer can tell you that the first thing to do if you want to build something is to make a blue-print.

---

* One reason why Marxism as a system of philosophy has not prospered in England and America is that we are not given to kidding ourselves about the sympathetic intentions of the universe. No system of philosophy has prospered among us. Our important works from Bacon to Bertrand Russell are expressions of skepticism and studies of scientific method. In this we are merely more advanced than the Germans and Russians, farther away from primitive superstition. The idea in which Marxism grew up that the Germans were "theoretical," the French "practical," etc., is erroneous. The greater "theoreticalness" of the Germans was simply their persistence in the forlorn attempt to make theories which, while explaining facts, would satisfy other

Specify what you are going to build. And be guided, moreover, from the first strokes of the pencil, by a consideration of the materials at your disposal. This does not mean, of course, that a scientific socialist should ignore the creativeness of future evolution, or go foolishly into the details of an earthly paradise. He should, indeed, know that there will be no earthly paradise. Nor does it mean that science in general, when concerned with human society, can have the exactitude of physics or astronomy—or even of agronomics or expert stockbreeding. It does mean that when proposing to build a new society a scientific mind would raise the question what qualities in the material, human nature, can be relied upon to make it function successfully and hold together. Even the "utopian" socialists, Marx's predecessors in the early nineteenth century, had raised this question and attempted to answer it. Robert Owen began his career with a series of essays designed to prove that man's moral character is wholly due to external circumstances, and that given the proper environment,

passions besides a passion to have the facts explained. Marx shared this background of German culture, so humbly absorbed by the Russians, and the effort of the Bolsheviks to put it over on us in the twentieth century as a super-scientific metaphysics should properly have been answered with a laugh.

The sentence above, "They have no ideal to realize . . . ," provides perhaps the best refutation of those who, in the effort to hold up Marx's philosophy in the environment of modern science, have contrived to identify it with John Dewey's instrumental theory of knowledge. Nobody who believed in that theory could conceivably have written such a sentence.

especially in early life, he will be as just, reasonable and intelligent as a co-operative commonwealth demands. Saint-Simon relied upon a new and more brotherly-intelligent kind of religious feeling to accomplish the required change. Fourier wrote a whole psychology to establish that a passion of social attraction, which he called *Unitéisme*, would harmonize all other passions, once conditions were established enabling us to function as our Maker had intended.

Marx never criticized these amateurish but obviously essential inquiries. He never said: "Well, let us look into this! What *is* there in human nature to give assurance that a society can really operate on the principle, 'From each according to his abilities, to each according to his needs'?"

To answer this question would have involved independent biological and psychological investigations. And Marx's system of philosophy made such investigations not only unnecessary, but, if you can believe it, impossible. Marx knew on philosophic grounds—which is to say, on faith—that the present society "tends by its own economic forces" toward a "higher form," and he knew that this higher form was indicated in a rough way by the utopian socialists. In order to "know" this, he had to make human nature a function of those economic forces. He had to "integrate" man, as he put it, in the economically evolving society:

DEFECTIVE BLUE-PRINTS 177

"The individual . . . has no real existence outside the milieu in which he lives, and in order to understand the true nature of man it is necessary to integrate him in society, in social life." "All history is nothing but a continual transformation of human nature."

That is the whole of Marx's contribution to this primary problem. And it is, of course, no contribution at all. These statements are advertised by his disciples as a wondrous prevision of modern psychology with its emphasis upon the social nature of the brain and nervous system. And they are that, incidentally. Marx was full of wondrous previsions. But their essential function in his system was to make unnecessary, and impossible, *any* independent science of psychology. Marx was on this head less scientific, not more so, than his predecessors. And there is consequently just as much utopianism in his idea of the future society as in theirs. He merely discusses it less often and more sketchily.

"The workers have no ideal to realize, they have only to set free the elements of the new society . . . ," and yet we may remark in passing that "in the higher phase of the Communist society . . . the limited horizon of capitalist right will be left behind entirely and society will inscribe upon its banners: *From each according to his abilities, to each according to his needs!*"

That in brief—and substantially in the words of Marx—is the Marxist's attitude toward his goal.

It must be remembered, of course, that this scheme

of revolutionary metaphysics was devised before the birthday of modern psychology, and while biology was still speculative, and sociology hardly imagined. It antedates Fechner and Herbert Spencer, Darwin and Huxley, and all the hard-headed fact-finders in these organic sciences. Marxism was in its own time and place a noble, as well as a fertile, intellectual construction. It does seem astonishing, however, that throughout these ninety years filled stupendously with advancing knowledge of life, and particularly of man's life and mind, not one Marxian has ever raised the simple question: Is human nature, as it has developed in the struggle for survival, sufficiently self-dependent and sufficiently co-operative, or sufficiently capable of self-dependence and malleable in a co-operative direction, so that a collectivization of property would actually lead to the society of the free and equal, the dying away of state power, the condition of felicity described in the formula: "From each according to his abilities, to each according to his needs"? Even Darwin's theory of species and of how their characters are determined did not provoke an inquiry on this head. It was only grabbed in as another evidence of the generality of upward evolution, a further proof that because of the nature of the universe—and never mind about man's nature!—we are bound to arrive at an earthly paradise. It shows how reckless of obtrusive fact is wish-fulfillment thinking, and how particularly dangerous when it puts on the name and aspect of hard sense and science.

THE FIRST EXPERIMENT

Since the scientific socialists were never scientific enough to ask that simple preliminary question about human nature, it is natural that their first experiment should surprise them with a most conclusive, bloody and implacable answer: No!

It is hardly necessary to go into the details of Stalin's murderous and hypocritical regime. It has been described as it looks to those who believed in the socialist ideal, and yet believe also in telling the bitter truth, by Andrew Smith in *I Was a Soviet Worker;* by Fred E. Beal, the Gastonia strike leader, in *Proletarian Journey;* by Boris Souvarine, First Secretary of the French communist party, in his monumental book, *Stalin;* by Victor Serge in *Russia Twenty Years After;* by Trotsky in *The Revolution Betrayed;* and above all, for Americans, by Eugene Lyons in his truthful and absorbing personal history, *Assignment in Utopia.*

That these truth-telling books by initiated minds are few, and are not always welcomed by publishers, need not cause any doubts of their reliability. After "socialization" was accomplished in Russia on paper, and after the revolution as a dynamic reality, a seizure of power by workers and peasants, was checkmated and its threat on the international field expressly withdrawn, the Western intelligentsia "went over" to Bolshevism almost in a body and with a very natural alacrity. For it is, alas, natural to an intelligentsia to want to believe with its mind in an extreme ideal, and yet be assured in its heart that the ideal holds no threat to present adjustments. This wholesale conversion, just because safely belated, was impetuous and intense, and it involved an immense investment both of emotion and of intellectual prestige. Its momentum therefore is great, and one finds it almost as hard now to get liberals to confront the cruel facts about Stalin's regime, as it was once to make the reactionary press print the glowing truth about Lenin and Trotsky and the workers' state. Facts, as Lenin said, are stubborn things; the only things equally stubborn are those who will not see them.*

Suffice it to say, then, for those who hold their eyes open, that together with that collectivization or nationalization of the means of production which was supposed to emancipate the working class, and therewith make "all society" free, and permit the state to die away, there has grown up as the substance of the state a caste or class of bureaucrats who have enslaved the proletariat more effectively than before, appropriating all

---

* The above paragraph was written before the Stalin-Hitler pact, but although no longer wholly true is still significant enough to stand.

DEFECTIVE BLUE-PRINTS 181

that can well be taken of the increasing product of their labor, and depriving them of every means of protest, and that besides enslaving the proletariat these bureaucrats have perfected the enslavement of "all society." Trotsky says boldly and truly, after describing socialism as "a classless society based upon solidarity and the satisfaction of all needs," that "in this fundamental sense there is not a hint of socialism in Russia." We might further say that there is not a hint of many of the liberties and equalities, to say nothing of the fraternities, which normally prevail under competitive capitalism. Indeed although there is in some respects a greater equality, there is far less liberty in Russia than there was under the semi-feudal regime of the tzars. As to "fraternity"—or, in Marx's wiser phrase, the rendering of "all the everyday relations of man to man perfectly intelligible and reasonable"—it is difficult to speak temperately. Bureaucratic usurpation and concealed class rule have made Russia, so far as she is public and articulate politically, a nation of informers, spies, hypocrites, lickspittles and mass-murderers. Her men and women of most noble and humane feeling are in jail, or in exile, or in concentration camps, or in hiding, or in traitors' graves, or cowed into absolute silence. Human relations have, I dare say, never on a large scale sunk so low. The deliberate murder by starvation of four to six million peasants in the name of a workers' and peasants' republic, and the wholesale execution in the name of the "complete triumph of socialism" of all the sincerest and most clear-sighted leaders of the movement toward socialism, are but high points in a total system based on lies and held erect by cruelty and terror.

Any mind realistically devoted to the original aims of socialism emerges from the library after reading the journals out of Stalin's Russia with the feeling recorded by the socialist mechanic, Andrew Smith, on leaving the country itself after his years of service there:

"As soon as we crossed the border it was as if we had suddenly been released from some dark, terrifying jail into the bright golden sunlight. The passengers broke out into lively conversation and ecstatic cries of joy, of freedom. They laughed, they cried, they sang."

It is impossible, after reading those journals, filled now these many months with shrieking rituals of obscene toadyism and insanely raging hate, to deny the extreme statement of Boris Souvarine in a recent article in *La Revue de Paris:*

"All respect for man having disappeared, life and human dignity having lost their value, nothing moderates the bestiality of the strong and the abasement of the weak. One sees no longer any limit to the savagery that has been unleashed."

After such statements from others who made sacrifices to the cause of communism in Russia, Fred Beal seems cool and moderate when he says:

DEFECTIVE BLUE-PRINTS 183

"The more I saw of Russia, the more convinced I became that not only the homeless children but all the common people of the country were a nuisance to the Soviet Government. . . ."

Fred Beal declined a frank invitation to a career of luxury and self-deception as a Soviet bureaucrat, in order to come home to the United States and, with a twenty-year prison sentence standing against him, tell the American workers the truth of what he saw. Although he has been criticized for publishing chapters of his book in the reactionary press, his book is honest, and will bring no ultimate reward to him but self-respect.

"I found," he says, "that the Stalinist road leads to calamity and darkness. But I am as convinced as ever that there is another road to a free and classless humanity, a road which is worth the quest, and which can be found only by minds liberated from the worship of false gods and by spirits strong enough to face the truth."

Beal says significantly, speaking of the radical books he read in youth: "I could not understand Karl Marx." This inability of clear-headed Americans to understand Karl Marx is wholly due to the fact that Marx was constrained by his German philosophical training to keep up a perpetual pretense that his simple practical plan for changing the world was an abstruse, theoretical understanding of how the world is changing itself. Beal's innocence of this metaphysical hokum was an essential part of his preparation for the task of telling American workers the truth about Soviet Russia. He is far more reliable, because of his naïve freedom to see a few un-intellectualized vital facts, than Trotsky is, with his colossal power to marshal all the facts, from the price of pig-iron to the forms of lyric poetry, within the framework of a romantic German philosophy.

In *The Revolution Betrayed,* more than in any other Marxian analysis of a concrete phase of history, the bare frame of this optimistic philosophy, this disguised mystic faith in a benign universe, begins to show through. Trotsky answers all the horrors to which the insurrection organized by him has led, with the assertion that socialism according to the Marxian theory was never supposed to be achieved in a single country, especially a backward one, and that the leaders of the Russian revolution thought of it only as a fuse to revolution in more advanced countries. He explains the absence of even a "hint of socialism" in Russia as due to her backward economy, low industrialization, low productivity of labor, lack of enough goods to go around, survival of "petty bourgeois psychology," etc., together with the pressure of world imperialism. He has very solemnly assured us (in an article in *Liberty*) that in America, because of her high industrial development, "communism, far from being an intolerable bureaucratic tyranny and individual regimentation, will be the means of greater individual liberty and shared abundance. . . .

Control over individual consumption—whether by money or administration—will no longer be necessary when there is more than enough of everything for everybody." Coming from a leader of the revolution, these statements are impressive, and I think Trotsky's Marxian analysis of the Soviet society in *The Revolution Betrayed* is a prodigious feat of intellect. The amount of free and fluid judgment he achieves within the framework of a rationalistic metaphysics is amazing—a tribute to his dexterity and the ingenuity of old Hegel. His sustained sense of human society as a process rather than a thing—the real wisdom concealed under the cant about "dialectic"—is also admirable. I find much truth too in his concrete demonstration of the results of Russia's backwardness. The idea of capitalist encirclement and the war danger, used by Stalinists to "blackmail the intellectuals and keep down the workers," as James T. Farrell truly says, is used by Trotsky with honesty and a true sense of its significance.

As to his essential thesis about Russia, however, I remain unconvinced. It is an exaggeration, in the first place, to say that the Russian revolution was always thought of by its leaders only as an initiator of world revolution. In his most vigorous polemic against those who maintained that proletarian action should have been postponed in October because Russia was not yet "ripe" for socialism, Lenin never mentions the world revolution, or the idea that socialism in Russia had to wait upon it. He says:

"How utterly mechanical is that idea which they learned by heart during the development of western European social democracy, that we in Russia have not yet grown up to socialism, that we lack—as various learned gentlemen among them express it—the objective economic premises for socialism. . . .

"If the creation of socialism demands a definite level of culture (although nobody can say just exactly what that definite level is) then why can we not begin by winning with a revolution the premises for that definite level of culture, and then afterward on the basis of the workers' and peasants' power and the soviet structure, set out to catch up to the other peoples? . . ."

Trotsky is, of course, wholly right in insisting that Lenin's Marxian policies demand the continued support of world revolution. He is wrong, however, in my opinion, when he implies that Lenin's hopes would not have been tragically disappointed by the developments in Russia even as an isolated proletarian state.

In the second place, Trotsky offers no real proof, except the tenets of the dialectic philosophy, that the sole decisive cause within Russia of the failure of socialist hopes is her backward technique of production. Like all true Marxians he builds that fact into, or up under, all the failures in every phase of the national life. And like all true Marxians, in doing this he ignores the very existence of the hereditary nature of man. No independent psychological or biological problems exist for him. Developments that to the most ordinary shrewd good sense reveal a conflict between Marxian theory and the average attributes of human nature, are attributed by him to survivals in a backward country of a "petty bourgeois psychology." The Marxian romantic idealization of the proletariat—based on no study of its character, based solely on its metaphysical position in the dialectic schema as the progressive factor in an upward-going contradiction—becomes almost a willful blindness in this book. The book is indeed "saturated" with optimism.

To my more skeptical and yet far from pessimistic mind, it seems obvious that if the socialist idea of a free and equal co-operative commonwealth emerging from the dictatorship of the proletariat were a practical one under an economy of abundance, we should find under an economy of scarcity some lame approximation to it. Instead of the germ of the society of the free and equal we find in Russia the perfect fruit of the totalitarian state. We find that national ownership of all wealth-producing capital makes it possible for a shrewd politician who gets hold of the state power to exercise a more absolute tyranny over the lives and minds of men than has been seen before. To the powers of an old-line political despot, he adds those of an apotheosized factory boss, and those of an armed Pope, an absolute censor of all printed or audibly spoken wish or opinion. And we find that this concentrated power is used, as indeed in the long run such power must be used, to restore in disguised forms the old system of class exploitation. That, it seems to me, is an already obvious lesson of the Russian revolution.

You can of course reply that the new bureaucracy and their privileges developed as rapidly as the process of collectivization, so that in reality "Socialism was never tried in Russia." The same thing is often said about Christianity, and I suppose always will be. There are people whose greatest need in life is a lost cause to believe in. And a lost cause surrounded by an edifice of scientifically plausible wish-fulfillment metaphysics, a kind of socio-economic Talmud in which to enjoy the delights of intellectual superiority and endless disputation, will unquestionably live forever. To a practical mind, however, the fact that after a completely successful revolution led by extreme and audacious Marxists, it proved impossible to show a "hint" of the authentic goal of Marxism, can only suggest a drastic reconsideration—or rather, since that is the lamentable fact about it, a belated preliminary consideration of the goal.

REVISIONS OF THE AIM

I said that there is just as much utopianism in Marx's ideal as in that of his predecessors. I will illustrate it with the following casual remark:

"Socialism will abolish both architecture and barrow-pushing as professions, and the man who has given half an hour to architecture will also push the cart a little until his work as an architect is again in demand. It would be a pretty sort of socialism which perpetuated the profession of barrow-pushing."

Other phrases which reveal the dream Marx had in mind are these:

"Leap from the kingdom of necessity to the kingdom of freedom"; "End of pre-history" and beginning of truly human history; Disappearance of "the enslaving subordination of the individual under the division of labor"; Disappearance of "the opposition between manual and intellectual labor"; Disappearance of "the contradiction between city and country"; "Labor becomes not only a means of life, but the highest desire of life"; "From each according to his abilities, to each according to his needs"; "An association which will exclude classes and their antagonisms"; "The practical relations of everyday life [will] offer to man none but perfectly intelligible and reasonable relations to his fellow men and to nature"; "In a society in which the motive for stealing has been done away with . . . the teacher of morals would be laughed at who tried solemnly to proclaim the eternal truth: Thou shalt not steal!"

All these aspirations, natural to anyone in a mood of wholesale revolt against the irrationality and meanness of human civilization, were lumped together by the Marxists, and for no other reason but that they are obviously unattainable under present conditions, were asserted to be the necessary end-products of an evolving technique of production. And for good measure Marx added the early Christian or anarchist idea of getting along without any government. It was first said, I believe, by the Anabaptists in the sixteenth, and the Diggers in the seventeenth century, that if property were held in common, no government would be necessary. And Marx, while telling us what a universe rising eternally of its own motion "from the lower to the higher" must ultimately arrive at, quite properly threw in this happy prospect too:

"There will no longer be political power, properly speaking, since political power is simply the official form of the antagonism in civil society."

Most of these formulae, if seriously considered in the light of present-day knowledge about human nature, can be thrown out offhand as fantastic. It hardly required the failure of the Russian revolution to inform modern minds that "labor" will never become, in the majority of mankind, the "highest desire of life"; that the opposition between manual and intellectual labor will never disappear, nor that between city and country; that no amount of collectivization can remove the division of labor or the subordination of the individual entailed by it; that the slogan "from each according to his abilities, to each according to his needs" is almost as utopian as the Golden Rule; that the conception of a "leap from the Kingdom of Necessity to the Kingdom of

DEFECTIVE BLUE-PRINTS 191

Freedom" is but a translation into this-worldly terms of the Christian myth of the resurrection; that the dream of man's having none but "perfectly intelligible and reasonable relations to his fellow men and to nature" is also not of this world. And if there is a more preposterous notion in the history of religion than that of the "scientific socialists" that when the gigantic mechanism of a concentrated capitalist industry is taken over by a proletarian state, and the attempt made to operate it on a basis of revolutionary justice, the state will immediately begin to "die away," I do not know where it is to be found. It was only by not thinking about these things that shrewd and hard-headed realists like Marx and Lenin managed to believe that they believed in them.

Our first step, then, must be to eliminate from our conception of the future society all those elements which require a belief in miracles, whether at the hands of the Divine Spirit or the Technique of Production. After that is done, we shall still find that we have in hand a perfectly thoughtless combination of two opposing political principles which, if pushed to an extreme, are incompatible. And we shall find that they are not only pushed to an extreme by Marxists, but pushed to the absolute. The Jeffersonian ideal of freedom and rank individualism and as little government as possible arose in, and according to Marx's own ways of thinking might seem properly to belong to, an agrarian society without highly developed industries or big cities. The development of these cities and industries has, at any rate, steadily forced this system into the background, and advanced into its place a system which stresses instead co-operativeness, and governmental regulation for the good of all. Marxism ignores this vital contrast and this momentous change, one of the most momentous in the history of political thought.

Marxism simply tosses into its pot at the end of the rainbow of future history all the ideals in both systems. And as though that were not utopian enough, it decrees that each and all are destined to be realized in as extreme a form as they can be conceived. Jefferson's shrewd and skeptical ideal of very little government becomes in Marx's believing mind the total disappearance of the state. The healthy notion supported by Lincoln that a man is entitled to the product of his labor is dismissed by Marx as "bourgeois." In the society to which the dictatorship of the proletariat inevitably conducts, his dialectic faith assures us, men will not receive according to their labor, but according to their needs. In my opinion anyone who, contemplating the results of the Russian revolution, can still dwell believingly in these myths of the absolute ideal, is unwilling to learn and unfit to teach. It is not a matter for emotion, whether of loyalty or despair. It is not a question, as Trotsky

DEFECTIVE BLUE-PRINTS 193

thinks, of "being frightened by defeat," or "holding one's position." It is a question of moving forward or being stuck in the mud. No mind not bold enough to reconsider the socialist hypothesis in the light of the Russian experiment can be called intelligent.

Russia's political ideals, during her ten years of violent industrialization, have passed in fevered form through the very development upon which ours spent a century. The freedom-individuality-and-less-government element has been forgotten, or deliberately withdrawn from circulation, and the co-operation-and-state-regulation element tends to be presented as though it were the single aim for which the revolution had been fought. Lenin's writings in the months preceding the October revolution were filled, as we have seen, with such expressions as these:

"One must *build* democracy directly, from the bottom, on the initiative of the masses themselves, and with their active participation in the *entire* life of the state, without 'supervision' from above, without officialdom. . . ." "Abolish the police, the bureaucracy and the standing army. Create a *militia* consisting of the whole people, women included, generally and universally armed. This is the practical business which should be launched without delay. The more initiative, variety, daring, creativeness are brought into play by the masses, the better."

Only a few years after those lines were written, Mr. René Fülöp Miller was able with but his usual exaggeration to attribute to Bolsheviks as such a belief that "the collective-impersonal is alone real and the separate existence of the single individual is an illusion," and the intention to "confiscate human dignity" and "turn all free reasonable beings into a horde of will-less automatons." And with the achievement of "complete collectivization," Mr. Fülöp Miller's horror story has come almost true. The freedom-and-individuality part of the socialist ideal has so completely dropped from view that even a transplanted American like Anna Louise Strong can solemnly reproach me that I fail to understand what is going on in Russia because I have not learned the art of "collective thinking."

One of the first problems for a new and more scientific social movement is to effect an adjustment between these two conflicting parts of the socialist ideal. It might have been deduced by a process of meditation, if anybody had done any meditating on these subjects, that the concept of extreme individualism is in conflict with that of extreme co-operativeness. The Russian experiment provokes the further query: To what extent is the principle of equality, vigorously applied, incompatible with a vigorous assertion of personal freedom? The resurrection of the death penalty for theft after all wealth-producing property has been "socialized" must induce some reflection, it seems to me, beyond the remark that Russia's wealth production is not high. It might well serve as a symbol of the thinking socialists have still to do.

If life is to have dignity and richness, the principles of freedom and individualism must be sacredly preserved. That they arose in a pre-industrial era, and will be difficult to cherish in an industrial one, only makes this issue the more pressing. But if life is to flourish in an age of machinery and mass production, there must also be a new co-operativeness, one involving a new degree of discipline and subordination to the collective purpose, and to that end more state control than would have been good sense in the time of Jefferson.

One cannot, of course, revise his aim completely in independence of his definition of the conditioning facts, or his program of action. Tentatively, however, we might sum up our revision of the socialist ideal in the light of science and the Russian experiment as follows:

1. Instead of being attributed as an end-term to an omnipotent process of historic evolution, the ideal should be regarded as a purpose in the minds of those who strive to reach it.

2. Problems of being and of universal history arising from this situation should be acknowledged to exist, but not solved by the device of pretending to know what is not known.

3. The various components of the ideal should be analyzed and considered separately.

4. Those obviously fantastic in the light of modern biological and psychological knowledge, to say nothing of modern common sense, should be thrown out.

5. None of those remaining should be conceived as absolute.

6. The incompatibility between the liberty-individuality principle and the collective co-operation principle should be adjusted, where necessary, by mutual concessions.

7. We must surrender to co-operation, and the attending state control, as much of our individual freedom as is indispensably necessary to the operation of a complicated wealth-producing machinery.

8. We must guard with eternal vigilance the rest.

10

TRUTH IN THE MARXIAN WORLD-VIEW

ALTHOUGH Marx fell short of science, and even of practical good sense, in failing to define his aim, he did make an elaborate examination of existing facts and of the developments that led up to them. In this part of his system—the theory of history, I mean, and the analysis of capitalism—he made indubitable contributions to science. He made discoveries and uncovered points of view that a more mature effort to change the social system will have to cling to. It is important to sift them out from what he felt obliged to read into history and the capitalist system in accordance with the dictates of his philosophy.

If you say that Marx first realized the major role played in history by the developing technique of production, you will be wholly right. And that discovery was momentous enough to institute an epoch in historiography, and place Marx among the immortals. But Marx was not content to say that, and neither are the

Marxians. They say that the course of human history is "determined by" the developing technique of production. And if you ask them: "What do you mean? Do not ideas and political institutions have anything to do with it?" they say: "Oh yes, they have a *retroactive* influence, but they themselves are the results of economic factors, which are thus the ultimate causes." Or they say: "Oh yes, ideas and institutions may *accelerate* the historic process, but they can not affect its course." Or they say: "Oh yes, ideas and institutions may determine the *course* by which history arrives at its goal, but they cannot determine the goal." Or they say: "Oh yes, ideas and institutions may have an influence, but *in the long run* the economic forces prevail." All of which is, of course, pure theological boloney. Ideas are just as much the cause as the result of changes in the technique of production; you cannot accelerate a complicated process without changing it; if you change the course by which history travels, you have changed history, for history has no "goal." As for "the long run," it has no meaning—all history is a long run.

The reason why this tangle of casuistries has arisen—and you could fill a five-foot shelf with it—is that Marx is trying to prove that human societies, like every other essential reality in a dialectic universe, are evolving "from the lower to the higher," and that the developing technique or "forces" of production can be relied on to carry any and all human societies from savagery, through barbarism, feudalism, capitalism, to the co-operative commonwealth.

Marx gave plausibility to his faith in these "material forces," just as Hegel had his faith in the Divine Spirit, by making their control immanent in the activities of men, not transcendent of them.

"History," he says, "is nothing but the activity of man in pursuit of his ends."

Which sounds entirely matter-of-fact and scientific—but to that he adds:

"Man makes his own history, but he does not make it out of the whole cloth; he does not make it out of conditions chosen by himself, but out of such as he finds at hand."

And to that again:

"By virtue of the simple fact that every generation finds at hand the forces of production acquired by an earlier generation . . . there arises a connection in human history, and the history of mankind takes form and shape."

And to that finally:

"I have added as a new contribution the following propositions: 1—That the existence of classes is *bound up in certain phases of material production;* 2—that the class struggle leads necessarily to the dictatorship of the proletariat; 3—that this dictatorship is but a transition to the abolition of all classes and the creation of a society of the free and equal." [Italics mine.]

Thus although man "makes" history, its continuity is written by the forces of production, and its "form and shape"—most notably the shape of things to come—are determined by these forces which man "finds at hand." That is the Marxian theory of history set forth by Marx himself—in quotations assembled, to be sure, from various places. It may be summarized thus:

Men make their own history, but they make it in material conditions that are continually given in advance; class relations inhere in these material conditions; therefore the class struggle, which is the dialectic essence of "all history," leads, regardless of men's choice or consciousness although through their acts, to the communist society.

Thus Marx was able to endorse without qualification a commentator of *Das Kapital* who wrote:

"Marx only troubles himself about one thing; to show by rigid scientific investigation, the necessity of successive determinate orders of social conditions, and to establish, as impartially as possible, the facts that serve him for fundamental starting points. For this it is quite enough, if he proves, at the same time, both the necessity of the present order of things, and the necessity of another order into which the first must inevitably pass over; and this all the same, whether men believe or do not believe it, whether they are conscious or unconscious of it. Marx treats the social movement as a process of natural history, governed by laws not only independent of human will, consciousness and intelligence, but rather, on the contrary, determining that will, consciousness and intelligence."

It is folly to ignore the crass superstition at the heart of this theory. Marx's much-touted "materialism" was not an advance from Hegel's religious metaphysics toward a scientific empiricism. It was a reversion from the primitive animism of Hegel to a fetichism that is still more primitive. Hegel, I mean, put his faith in a reasonable, purposive spirit conceived to reside within, or be revealed by, the sticks and stones of which the world seems to be made; Marx attributed his reasonable purpose to the sticks and stones. Out of the indubitable fact that historic evolution is *conditioned* by the raw materials and technique of production—which really sets stern limits to the possibilities of an earthly paradise—he manufactured an optimistic philosophy according to which historic evolution is *determined* by the raw materials and technique of production, and determined in such a direction that an earthly paradise is sure.*

---

* It has been a fashion recently, seeing that Marx was an ardent propagandist and preacher of struggle, to deny that he held this metaphysical belief. Some people who adore him, or adore the Talmud that has been made out of his writings, insist that he was in reality a "scientific pragmatist." Marx was just as much a pragmatist as his master Hegel was, no more and no less. Hegel had ways of reconciling his faith in the Divine necessities of history with a gospel of duty and sacrifice—most esoteric among them the sophistical aphorism of Schelling that "freedom is necessity conscious of itself." Marx added no word on that head to what he had learned in the Hegelian school.

A MATTER-OF-FACT INTERPRETATION OF HISTORY

I go into these abstruse matters because I think there is danger that, in the recoil from the Russian fiasco, we shall throw over what is hard and valid, instead of what is soft and false, in the Marxian system. It has long been customary in scholarly deprecations of Marxism to say that Marx did well to emphasize the conditioning influence of economics and productive technique, but that he *over*emphasized it. With that the scholar feels free to return to the hortatory mode of teaching history. Marx did not overemphasize the conditioning influence of economics and technique, he underemphasized it. He was too German-philosophical to confront the real implication of it, the limits that it placed upon his romantic faith in an undefined millennium.

To believe in a reasonable and humane ideal to which society may be steered by a co-operative effort, and yet believe that an unflinching recognition of conditioning facts is essential to the success of the effort, begets a cool-purposed and relentlessly hard-visioned, but not bigoted, brutal or cynical condition of mind. To believe that society is tending "by its own economic forces" toward your humane ideal, and that a *knowledge of this objective fact* is what primarily distinguishes you from your opponents, does beget bigotry, brutality and a peculiarly serene cynicism. It enables Marxian writers to enjoy in the name of science all the privileges of the self-righteous, and in the name of rational understanding, to indulge in prejudiced contempt. And it enables Marxian statesmen to outdo all princes in the fervor of their Machiavellianism. It is a main cause of the unparalleled savagery and large-scale hypocrisy of the Bolshevik party in its decline—unparalleled by anything in the history of revolutions. The power-thirsty primitive beast in man's nature has burst through and possessed these latter-day Bolsheviks not only in spite of socialist ideals, but with the help of those ideals. For ideals in the Marxian system are not standards of conduct, nor even purposes of will, but "mental symptoms" of an impending material change for the better, of which the Marxist's knowledge is absolute and his opponent's ignorance abysmal. The state of mind was epitomized by Bukharin, in justifying some preliminary massacres of the Stalin machine: "We must be ruthless because the sword of history is in our hand."

In rejecting the naïve notion that the material world is dialectically determined from the lower to the higher, we must retain the wisdom linked up with it—the unremitting awareness of change, and very profound change, in social relations as history proceeds. In rejecting the superstition of an immanent deity called Forces of Production, who in some mysterious way has the last word as to where history is going, we must retain the sterner truths that lie under that. Historic changes, profound as they may be, are rigidly limited and conditioned by economic factors, and at the bottom by the raw materials and developing technique of production. They are still further limited by biological and psychophysiological factors which, as Marx quite failed to realize, are hereditary and thus also "found at hand" by each new generation. Frederick Engels—significantly enough, at the graveside of Marx—summed up most simply this surviving truth of Marxism:

"Human beings must have food, drink, clothing and shelter first of all, before they can interest themselves in politics, science, art and religion."

They must have it, and in the aggregate, whether consciously or unconsciously, they tend to sense this fact and act accordingly. A wise historian will not be deluded by what men say, or even think, where it runs counter to this basic tendency of their actions. A scientific socialist will not move against this conditioning factor nor preach against it. Taking man, the wealth-producing biological animal, as he is, he will seek rather to inform his mind than to reform his motives. Enlightenment and non-sectarian organization will be the basic instruments, not exhortation and conversion to a faith. Hardheaded skeptical studious matter-of-factness will be the mood. To combine that with inflexible adherence to an ideal aim, is the essential ethic, the problem in equilibrium, for all who want to join hands in an effective effort toward a freer and more equal society. This equilibrium has not often been attained, I think, outside the socialist and syndicalist movements, and it has not been attained within these movements except by a few minds, predominantly Latin or Anglo-Saxon, who have instinctively accepted the hard sense and rejected the romantic philosophy in the Marxian system.

AN ECONOMICS THAT MEANS BUSINESS

There is a great deal of hard sense in the Marxian analysis of capitalism. The very concept of profound historic change in economic relations which makes the word "capitalism" mean so much to us, by contrast both to feudalism and to some new set of relations conceivable in the future, is due to Marx. To him also is due the adequate realization that in one respect economic relations did not change with the passage from feudalism to capitalism—that is, the exploitation of the labor of a subject class. His dialectic philosophy, combining with his revolutionary passion, led him to see long before others the crucial practical flaw in our way of producing and distributing wealth. We all discuss now as our chief problem that question of getting "purchasing power"—which is Marx's "surplus value"—back into the hands of the producers from whom it is taken by the owners of the instruments of production. We all realize that this problem has been rendered more urgent by the gradual disappearance of foreign markets. We know the relation between the search for foreign markets and international war. We know the special problems created by the concentration of ownership in few hands, another development whose scope and importance were first grasped by Marx. You might indeed say that Marx discovered the subject-matter of modern political and social thought.

Another prodigious thing he did was to build up all these newly discovered facts, together with much else, into a world-philosophy for proletarians. Almost every new major discovery of science—every newly discovered science, at least—has had built upon it a total way of looking at the world. Marx built one upon the science of economics. The result is a little naïve and incomplete by comparison with the great systems of philosophy, but it is also, by comparison with them, emotionally unique. The very conception of a philosophy for the lowest class —of putting the universe, so to speak, at the service of the slaves—is so exhilarating an event in the stuffy and pompous history of metaphysical speculation that it gives Marx's name a flavor of distinction like that of the really great philosophers. Although "Marxists" will be the last to acknowledge it, this aesthetic achievement, as impractical as the erection of a cathedral and having as little relation to the progress of science, will survive as one of his most lasting monuments in history.

The world is full of more or less valid criticisms of *Das Kapital* as an inquiry into the method of wealth production prevailing in our modern era, and its tendencies of development. But few economists are philosophic enough to make the fundamental criticism—namely, that *Das Kapital* is not such an inquiry, and that no such inquiry was ever made by Marx. *Das Kapital* is an investigation of the question: How can the facts and methods of production and distribution prevailing in our era be made to illustrate a dialectic philosophy according to which all totalities are in process of evolution toward higher forms by way of inner conflict and self-contradiction? The philosophy, and its application to history as a whole, had been completely worked out and finished fifteen years before Marx published the first volume of *Das Kapital*, many years before he ever went to work on it. Lenin himself says that Marx's views were mature in 1844 and '45. They were mature theoretically then, and in the years immediately following they had a good practical application. The communists in the revolutions of 1848 did not stumble or fail through need of the Marxian analysis of capitalism. There is no such need. The essential practical outcome of the analysis of capitalism is known as soon as you have read the Communist Manifesto. All that is not known is how ingeniously it will be arrived at, what wealth of concrete factual material will be woven in with its demonstration, how many important lights will be shed on economic problems in the by-going. An explorer has, of course, a right to set sail from where he will, and the fact that Marx was a Hegelian does not invalidate the specific discoveries that his mystic wish-fulfillment metaphysics led him to make. But it does invalidate the pretense of the whole system to be empirical. It makes the work of economists who criticize it without regard to its true nature ineffectual, and a great waste of time. *Das Kapital* is an attempt to read a revolutionary religious faith in the economic under-structure of history at large into the mode of production prevailing in the present phase of history. It is not economic science, but economic metaphysics with some scientific wisdoms wound up in it.

What I have said, then, about the analysis of history in general applies to the analysis of capitalism. We have to reject the pretense of Marx to have penetrated the "outward disguises," constituted by the prices at which things actually sell on the market, "into the internal essence and inner form of the capitalist process of production." There is no such internal essence, no such inner form; there are facts and valid or invalid generalizations of them. And we have to reject the romantic philosophical notion of Marx that in pointing out the *im-*

practicalities of capitalism when goods become abundant, laying bare a problem for mankind to solve, he was discovering *"contradictions"* in capitalism indicative of the manner in which a universe obligingly interested in such contradictions was going to solve the problem. But in rejecting these mystical and soft parts of the Marxian economics, we must not let go of its great innovation into economic thinking, a sense of the past existence and future possibility of profound change. And we must cling to its hard-headedness about business facts, its driving home of the necessity, before we can begin to expatiate about cultural progress or even survival, of solving the basic problem which it poses.

Note: My treatment of Marx, especially in this concluding section, must necessarily seem cursory to his studious disciples. I have criticized his system at length in the following works: *Marx and Lenin, the Science of Revolution; Artists in Uniform,* Part III, reproduced also in *The Making of Society,* a sociological anthology published by the Modern Library; An Introduction to *Capital and Other Writings,* also published by the Modern Library; *The Last Stand of Dialectical Materialism, A Study of Sidney Hook's Marxism;* and *The Seed of the Marxian Philosophy,* an article published in the *New International,* but designed to replace Chapter II in a new edition of *Marx and Lenin* to be entitled *Marxism—Science or Religion?*

11

THE ROLE OF PERSONALITIES

THE essence of the Marxian plan of action is, of course, the prosecution of the working-class struggle. But there is a preliminary practical question which nags many of us privately—the question whether large personal aims and dedications like that called socialism have any effect at all upon the historic process. Like other religions, philosophic Marxism solved this problem by convincing the believer that the external forces were on his side. In a dialectic universe the process of history is itself revolutionary; to have revolutionary aims and have true knowledge are, therefore, the same thing. "Our theories are programs-of-action." Moreover, the ultimate success of these programs-of-action is, for the true believer, "guaranteed." Lenin in his first pamphlet, written in 1895, showed how Marx had solved this problem for him. The Marxian idea of the historic necessity of higher social forms, instead of making him feel ineffectual, made him feel sure that he was on the winning side:

"The idea of historic necessity does not in the least undermine the role of personalities in history; history is all composed of the activities of persons, who are indubitable agents. The real question arising in an appraisal of the social activities of persons is: In what conditions are these actions guaranteed success? Where is the guarantee that this action will not remain a solitary deed drowned in a sea of contrary activities?"

Science knows no historic necessity of higher social forms, and to anyone abandoning metaphysical self-delusions, this question of the role of persons and the effectiveness of their actions is reopened. It is reopened with special poignancy for those who see that Lenin himself, after adhering to a line of social conduct with inflexible passion and flexible intelligence for thirty years from the date of that pamphlet, achieved well-nigh the opposite result from that which he thought "guaranteed." Setting out to create a labor republic in which the proletariat and therewith all society would be free, he bequeathed to history a totalitarian state in which all society, and therewith the proletariat, are enslaved to a degree unimagined by him. He had no better luck than his opponents who fought a war "to make the world safe for democracy." Hannibal in early youth took a vow of eternal hostility to the city of Rome. He stuck to that for thirty-odd years, and his biographer, concluding the story, says:

"The battle of Magnesia gave Rome the dominion of the eastern Mediterranean as that of Zama had given her the dominion of the western. . . . The life's work of Hannibal was over. He had created the Roman Empire."

Such facts, pressed home to thoughtful minds in these sad days, have given rise to some interesting but inconclusive books: Henry DeMan's *The Psychology of Socialism*, Karl Mannheim's *Ideology and Utopia*, Thurman Arnold's *Folklore of Capitalism*, Charles Beard's *The Discussion of Human Affairs*. They were anticipated in revolutionary literature by Georges Sorel, with his doctrine of the Social Myth. In my book *Marx and Lenin*, in which notwithstanding their false base in metaphysics I endorsed Lenin's policies as an essentially scientific system of revolutionary engineering, I was correspondingly intolerant of Sorel's idea that the socialist theories are myths rather than plans, that a revolutionary movement cannot be engineered, that "everything in it is unpredictable." I was intolerant of DeMan's idea that one could be a revolutionist without believing in the revolution, that "the present motive, not the future goal, is the sole essential." I still think these are sickly states of mind, and that it would be better, both for the revolution and for the person afflicted with them, if he would abandon the ideal which he considers utopian, and pursue some lesser aim that he believes can be realized. As I have shown in a previous chapter, many elements of the socialist ideal are utopian. They *are* social myths and should be abandoned. But even after that correction is made, there remains a vast difference between dedication to an aim which involves the historic growth of all society, and a personal effort to do something for oneself or one's community. The difficulty of prediction is more vast; the means of control run into conflict with the aim; there is greater hazard of proving not only futile, but in some unforeseen way, an obstacle to one's wish.

I find myself, in view of these facts, not only urging a more careful definition of the aims we have in view, but in my own mind falling back upon a thought with which, long before the Russian revolution gave such body to our hopes, I entered the socialist movement: that to participate in a struggle for those large aims, whether they be achieved or not, is to live a good life. It is, certainly, not good to struggle, as both Sorel and DeMan advocate, toward aims which you do not believe can be realized. That makes speech hollow and action weak. To lead others in such a struggle strikes me as demagogic. But to struggle toward aims that you know may or may not be realized, and find a part of your satisfaction in the superior keenness of a life edged and tempered by such struggle, seems a fair mixture of motives. It qualifies the rage of the zealot, but qualifies it with a tincture of personal morality which is often the chief lack in those who close all questions with an act of dogmatic belief. It is the only solution I can offer of the first problem to arise in the minds of revolutionists freed of the Marxian delusion, and aware also of the colossal failure of Lenin's Bolshevik party.

12

THE DOCTRINE OF CLASS STRUGGLE

A MORE urgent problem is as to the place a scientific movement would accord to the Marxian guiding principle of class struggle. To Marx the class struggle was not merely a fact, and its prosecution a method of progress toward socialism. It was the "inner essence" of all history, the mystic principle of dialectic evolution as it appears in the totality called society. All human activities, even the science of history itself, were to Karl Marx class activities. His own big work, *Das Kapital,* was not objective science, but a revolutionary act of "criticism" with a working-class bias. It was "truer" than the bourgeois economics only as the working class was the progressive class, the class destined in the dialectic process to overcome and replace the bourgeoisie. Lenin said in his outline of Marxism: "There can be no objective social science in a society torn by class struggle."

Such a statement, when deprived of its metaphysical foundation, is of course fantastic. Science is nothing but a determined effort to be dispassionate in establishing facts. Lenin himself had extraordinary gifts in establishing particular facts, and he made constant use of accepted generalizations. The statement that "there can be no objective social science in a society torn by class struggle" itself lays claim to objective truth. Except as laying such claim, it has no meaning and one could have no purpose in uttering it. Moreover it is so far-reaching and consequential a statement that only a very highly developed science could confirm it. It was effectively contradicted by another super-class dictum for which Lenin is famous: his statement, namely, that the working class did not of itself (and could not!) arrive at the socialist ideology, that "this had to be brought in by cultured representatives of the possessing classes." If these cultured representatives could so far abandon their class bias as to create a working-class ideology, why could they not abandon it just a little less, and arrive at some objective judgments of fact?

It is true that objective judgments about society are difficult to arrive at. This is because the scientist is a part of the material he examines, and occupies a particular position within it, one usually entailing passionate opinions. He can, however, roughly distinguish such opinions from ascertained facts. And he will certainly, if he believes in intelligence, be influenced by his very understanding of class interests to try to escape from their hot clutch and achieve opinions whose probability will be coolly objective and real.* On this act of self-understanding rests the hope that man may yet cope with the social problem as he has with the problems of physics and mechanics. We must not let the class struggle as a mystic principle interfere with that hope. Class struggles are facts among other facts, determinable and in some ways measurable, and whatever attitude we adopt to them we should adopt for reasons that are, so far as possible, objectively valid and can be verified.

FACTUAL THINKING

In another way the belief that class struggle is the "inner essence" of capitalist society vitiates the thinking of all confirmed Marxians. They permit themselves on principle to attribute attitudes and judgments to "the workers," the "working class," the "proletariat," which they well know are as a matter of statistical fact confined to little circles of militant revolutionists who have taken the position that the Marxian world-scheme allots to the workers. In times of revolutionary crisis when class divisions are accentuated, a majority of the workers does often tend toward this position, and that supports the Marxians in their conviction that their speech is valid about the "inner essence" all along. There is no inner

* A similar thing is said in the conclusion of Charles Beard's excellent little book, *The Discussion of Human Affairs*.

essence. It is a fact that the workers as a whole are usually not in the position or state of mind allotted to them by the Marxists. That they tend toward that position in times of revolutionary crisis is another fact. For purposes of valid discourse one of these facts is just as "true" as the other. We must have valid discourse. The class struggle is not a super-scientific dogma. It is a fact where it exists, and no inferences can be drawn from it where it does not. The idea that a better society can be arrived at by promoting the victory of the lower classes in the struggle, is a hypothesis, subject like other scientific hypotheses to the test of experiment.

RESPONSIBILITY IN ACTION

We must have not only valid discourse, but responsible action. It was his mystic faith that he was acting in accord with "inner essences" which enabled Lenin with a good conscience to seize power in the name of the working class, and feel sure that the working class would hold it. Such faith can move mountains, but it cannot make them stay. It is common just now, among thoughtful socialists, to say that the horrors of Stalinism have their root in Lenin's policies—the centralized party led by "professional revolutionists" acting in the name of the working class, and afterwards the suppression of other working-class parties, the one-party dictatorship. It is true that Stalinism has its root in those policies of

Lenin. But it is further true that those policies of Lenin have their root in the mystical philosophy of Karl Marx.

Throughout his life Lenin felt free to mean by the "workers"—except when analyzing transitory real facts for tactical purposes—not the then actually existing workers as a body, nor a majority of them, but an ideal essence demanded by the Marxian apotheosis of class. That made it easy in a crisis to attribute his Marxian policy to the workers, and in the name of the workers to suppress other less Marxian working-class parties. That made it easy, and indeed logically necessary, to believe that workers who opposed this policy, as in Kronstadt, were being "used" by other classes. Had Lenin regarded the class struggle merely as a fact, loose-edged and limited as all social facts are, and conceived of his policy of accentuating and organizing the workers' side of it, as a method by which he hoped to produce a workers' republic, he could not conscientiously—as he undoubtedly did—have suppressed other working-class movements.

To put it another way, had he known that he was conducting an experiment on the class-struggle hypothesis, he could not have coerced the working class, for that would destroy the value of the experiment. He believed that in the inner essence of things, he *was* the working class, he and his trained Marxian party, and if concrete members of the too actual working class of the moment failed to perceive it; history, the upward-going universe, the dialectic evolution of capitalism, would bring them to themselves. Stalin, the ruffian, is incidental; but Stalinism, the military suppression and exploitation of the workers by a totalitarian state controlled by a bureaucratic party calling itself proletarian, has its roots, not only in Lenin's power-policies, but in the religious belief in a benignly evolving universe which lay behind those policies.

AS TO ROSA LUXEMBURG

There is no doubt in my mind that Marx would in a similar crisis have applied his principles in substantially the way Lenin did. Believing that his policies represented the "historic mission" of the working class, he would have suppressed along with other classes those portions of the working class who failed to understand their mission.* I think that any bold and passionate man of action, filled with this unflinching belief, would have done the same thing. And I include among such "men of action" the chief revolutionary critic of Lenin's organizational policies, Rosa Luxemburg. At the begin-

* Marx's worshipers like to pretend that he was entirely "empirical." Even Engels says that he never deduced anything from the dialectic theory. A man who fervently believed that every totality in the world is in process of evolution, by inner conflict and its resolution, toward "higher forms," and that capitalist society is such a totality—a man who believed that and made no deductions from it, would be a fool such as nature rarely has produced.

ning of the century, she attacked in these words Lenin's conception of the way a social democratic party should be linked or connected with the spontaneous organizations of the working class:

"The Social Democracy is not linked or connected with the organizations of the working class, but is the movement of the working class itself. It can be nothing other than the imperious co-ordination of the will of the enlightened and fighting vanguard of the workers as contrasted with its different groups and individuals; this is, so to speak, a 'self-centralism' of the leading element of the proletariat, the majority rule of that element within its own party organization."

And after Lenin's victory in October 1917, she continued her criticism:

"The basic error of the Lenin-Trotskyist theory is simply this: that they set dictatorship, just as Kautsky does, over against democracy. 'Dictatorship or democracy'—that is the question both for the Bolsheviks and for Kautsky. Kautsky decides, naturally, for democracy . . . Lenin and Trotsky decide for dictatorship in opposition to democracy and, in so doing, for the dictatorship of a handful of individuals, that is, for dictatorship after the bourgeois fashion. Two opposite poles, both equally removed from the true socialist policy.
"When the proletariat seizes power, it cannot follow Kautsky's advice and renounce the job of carrying through a socialist transformation, under pretext of the 'unripeness of the country,' and devote itself merely to democracy, without committing treason to itself, to the International and to the Revolution. It is bound to and must without delay, in the most vigorous, unwavering

and thorough-going manner, take socialist measures in hand, hence exercise dictatorship—but dictatorship of the class, not of a party or clique; dictatorship of the class, that is, in the broadest publicity, with the active participation of the masses, in unlimited democracy."

Those words sound prudent today, and socialists who realize how naturally Stalinism has grown out of Lenin's principles are turning back to Luxemburg as a more reliable leader than Lenin. I think that Lenin was the more reliable leader because he had a more realistic foresight. He knew in advance what he would have to do in a power crisis, and he was prepared to do it. My assertion that Luxemburg, if confronted by the same crisis, would have done the same thing, or perhaps less successfully tried to, is not a psychoanalytic impertinence, but an inference from what she says:

The working class *"is bound to and must without delay, in the most vigorous, unwavering and thorough-going manner, take socialist measures,"* but it must take them as "a class," not "a party," and still less "a clique"; it must take them "in the broadest publicity," "with the active participation of the masses," "in unlimited democracy."

It is bound to and must—but suppose it doesn't! What are you going to do then? That is the real question, and it was never answered by Rosa Luxemburg. It could not be answered by her, because she was a "true believer" in the Marxian religion, and for a true believer such a question cannot arise. The proletariat—if the revolution is a real one—"is bound to and must," and what binds it is the mystic threads of the Hegelian logic. When the real proletariat, whose nature and propensities are to be learned, if at all, from biology and psychology, not logic —when the real proletariat fails to act "without delay, in the most vigorous, unwavering and thorough-going manner," as it usually will fail, is there much doubt what a mystic believer in its historic destiny, having the impatient and masterful will and mind of Rosa Luxemburg, will do? The doubt will hardly survive a survey of what she did do, even in peacetimes, as leader of the Polish and Lithuanian socialist parties.

The real question about class versus party, democracy versus centralism, masses versus leaders, the worker versus the intellectual, can only be raised by a person who understands that the Marxian idea of achieving socialism through working-class struggle and seizure of power is a hypothesis. He only is in a position, while himself vigorously promoting the revolution, to insist upon "the active participation of the masses," "unlimited democracy," etc. He only is prepared, if this participation fails, to see that the revolution, or his essential plan for it, has failed.

QUANTITATIVE ESTIMATES

Besides rendering discourse invalid and action irresponsible, a super-scientific faith in class division prevents one from taking an attitude of measurement toward these divisions, or observing the changes that occur in their depth and sharpness.

A vast amount of ink has been spilled by Marxians in futile discussion as to whether the misery of the proletariat has increased, whether the middle class has diminished, whether stock-holdings and the formation of a labor aristocracy have not essentially blurred this cleavage, and more recently, whether the separation of control from ownership has not altered the whole picture, whether elaborate power-driven machinery has not so largely replaced the industrial proletariat as to deprive it of coercive power. I call these discussions futile because, to a believer in the dialectic theory, the conclusion is foregone. No stock-holdings, labor-saving machinery, high union wages, increase of middle class, decreasing misery, or separation of control from ownership, *can* alter the fact that society is cleaving along the class line between capital and labor. In the absence of any other cleavage fruitful of revolution, that belongs among the attributes of Being-as-such. Society could not exist in a dialectic universe, could not be conceived as a totality, without having this

DOCTRINE OF CLASS STRUGGLE 225

progressive conflict within it as its essential nature.

Once that self-deceiving nonsense and the emotions attending it are abandoned, any intelligent mind must admit that all the above qualifications of the class-struggle principle are to some degree valid. As there is no adequate technique of measurement, it is difficult to estimate to what degree. But we can say this at least: *To a sufficient degree to account for the first negative result of the Russian Bolshevik revolution, its failure to engender revolutions in neighboring countries where capitalism was more advanced.**

Trotsky, adhering to orthodox Marxism—which he rightly calls a "philosophy of optimism"—has been satisfied to record this devastating fact, explain by it his own defeat and the rise of Stalinism, and then proceed to ad-

---

*The fact that the proletarian revolution broke out in a country where the "contradictions of capitalism" were unripe does not, strictly speaking, refute the Marxian theory—exactly because this is not a theory of concrete causes, but a philosophy of being in general. As Lenin and Trotsky have both pointed out, the theory relates to totalities, and you have only to make your totality larger—you have only to say "the capitalist world" instead of "a capitalist nation"—and you have a more generalized ripeness of contradictions which accounts for the revolution's *beginning* in any part of that world. Indeed, although I have never seen it quoted, Marx himself, in the earliest exposition of his philosophy, prepared against such a surprise as the Russian revolution. In *The German Ideology*, written in 1845, he said:

"All the collisions of history have their origin, according to our conception, in the contradiction between the productive forces and the form of intercourse. It is moreover not necessary, in order that it lead to collisions in a given country, for this contradiction to come to a head in that country itself. The competition with industrially more developed countries . . . suffices to create a similar contradiction even in countries with a less developed industry."

vocate a similar revolution in a similarly backward country, Spain, on the very same grounds—namely, that it will engender a revolution in a neighboring country where capitalism is more ripe. A prudent mind, committed neither to optimism nor to pessimism, but to an attitude of thoughtful experiment, could hardly be so blithe. Such a mind would feel bound to *explain* the total non-appearance of that world revolution whose swift inception had been so confidently banked upon when power was seized in Russia. For me it is mainly explained by those concrete mitigations of the class division in capitalist society which Trotsky's abstract philosophy prevents him from appraising. I do not conclude that in a general economic breakdown, a revolution led by the industrial proletariat in an advanced capitalist country is impossible. But I think it is unlikely.* It is far more likely that a theory-blinded minority, agitating for it, will provide the occasion for a seizure of power

* I not only hold this opinion myself, but I believe it to be held privately by a considerable number of those Bolsheviks (that is, "Trotskyists") who seem to be whole-heartedly agitating for a seizure of power. They are so confident in print, because they know there is no immediate danger of the American workers listening to them. Even so, a common-sense anxiety about what will *really* happen if they go after power, is sometimes to be detected in their writing. "The issue of destiny," says Maurice Spector in the *New International*, "is acquiescence with the course of the imperialists, or *with all its hazards*—the proletarian revolution." The italics are mine. The note struck by them was not heard before the Russian revolution failed and its failure gave currency among revolutionists to the scientific criticism of Marx's determinist philosophy.

on the Stalin-Hitler plan. This kind of danger was foretold in Trotsky's audacious announcement in the winter of 1936 that the French proletarian revolution had begun. His glaring mistake was the underestimation of Stalin's power. And that too was due to his habit of schematic thinking based on the class struggle as a mystic dogma, or in his own phrase, a "law of all laws." There is no law of all laws.

THE DOCTRINE OF THE STATE

One of the most purely theological products of the Marxian super-scientific conception of class struggle is the so-called theory of the state. It is obvious to perception that any state, and above all one based upon the elective principle, fulfills a variety of functions. In many respects it serves the whole public as equitably as economic conditions permit. Even in a millennium there would be no need to revolutionize the Post Office. A large body of judicial decisions, executive measures and acts of Congress have the same character. How large a body, and how far capable of extension, has not been determined. By Marxians such a question cannot be asked, for they think the state also has an "inner essence," and that scientific definition consists in giving this inner essence an emotive name. The state, they say, is "the executive committee of the ruling class"—and that is at least consistent with their opinion that the inner essence of society and all history is class struggle.

Here again there has been much futile discussion, all of which can be thrown out of the window as based on a medieval notion of what it means to define. One may characterize the state for purposes of violent revolution as an executive committee of the ruling class, but for general purposes, and above all wherever the validity of that particular purpose comes in question, characterization must give way to definition. And a definition is not an intuition of abstract essences, much less a denunciation disguised as such, but a generalization of concrete facts.

Lenin's pamphlet, *State and Revolution,* in which an emotive characterization poses, with the aid of Marxian theology, as a definition of the state, was his prelude to the revolution of October 1917. It contains, in addition to that pseudo-definition, all of Lenin's most utopian predictions of what would follow a proletarian overthrow and "smashing" of the bourgeois state. The overthrow followed, the bourgeois state was smashed, and the end-result is approximately the opposite of all those beautiful predictions. In view of this it seems a mere counsel of prudence to abandon, together with those utopian predictions, the theological mode of thinking underlying them. Instead of proclaiming the "class essence" of the state, ask the simple practical questions: To what degree, in what departments, under what circumstances, with how universal a necessity, does the state function as a weapon of the ruling class?

Stalin and the fascists have shown us what the state, when really handled as a naked weapon, can become. They have made such distinctions as that of the "exploitative," "arbitrative" and "administrative" state, as employed by Stephen Raushenbush in his informing book, *The March of Fascism,* of interest and importance to everybody. Let us stop talking theology and join in the conversation of intelligent human beings.

REVOLUTIONARY JESUITISM

As unscientific as their attitude toward the state is the Jesuitical attitude toward morals which the Bolsheviks base upon their dialectic super-science. Unfortunately, in the case of both the Jesuits and the Bolsheviks rough common sense, in rejecting this attitude with disgust, has tagged it merely as a doctrine that "the end justifies the means." An end is frequently the sole justification of a means, and intelligent conduct requires freedom to decide whether this justification exists in a particular case or not. A belief that winning power for the Church of Rome justifies *any* means, regardless of the Christian ideals of the church; a belief that winning power for the communist party justifies *any* means, regardless of the ideals of communism; these are more adequate definitions of Jesuitism.

"Follow the other man's course to your own goal" was the doctrine of Loyola that made his Society of Jesus so monstrous an outrage to men of honest good sense. A conspirative organization—"militant, strictly centralized, aggressive, dangerous alike to enemies and allies," as Trotsky has said—the Jesuits made systematic use of crime and hypocrisy, ostensibly to spread the religion of Jesus, but in reality to restore power to Rome. Where wealth and fine garments seemed helpful, they put them on; where poverty was in spiritual vogue, they came in tatters and with bleeding feet. They were equally elastic in putting on and taking off ideas. They had no principles but power for the organization. Since Trotsky himself has acknowledged that, formally or psychologically, "the Bolsheviks appear in relation to the democrats and social democrats of all hues as did the Jesuits in relation to the peaceful ecclesiastical hierarchy," it is needless to argue this parallel.

The Stalinists, who have removed to far horizons the original Bolshevik goal of a society of the free and equal, and gone in for party power on any terms, are not only formally, but in the substance of their work, a reincarnation of the Jesuits. When these zealots of organizational obedience, acting on orders from Moscow, drape themselves in the American flag, and applaud Roosevelt, and form "leagues for peace and democracy," and shout for "free speech," "free assemblage," "free labor unions," they are fulfilling to the letter the maxim of Loyola: "Follow the other man's course to your own goal." When they begin suddenly to denounce Roosevelt and shout, "Keep America out of this war against Germany," they are doing the same thing. The goal is ostensibly the socialist society, but in reality it is world power for Stalin's totalitarian state. Anybody who does not know this does not want to know it.

What is not so well known is the degree to which Lenin and Trotsky, and their belief in the Marxian dialectic religion, are responsible for this policy of public hypocrisy. They taught that decent social conduct, impossible in a world divided into classes, will become universal in a classless society. And since the world is traveling toward that classless society by a process of class struggle, any conduct is good now which is helpful in the struggle. Trotsky has recently made this dangerous mental attitude extremely clear. He asks whether "lying and violence 'in themselves' warrant condemnation," and answers:

"Of course, even as does the class society which generates them. A society without social contradictions will naturally be a society without lies and violence. However, there is no way of building a bridge to that society save by [class struggle, to which lies and violence are necessary].... The morality of the proletariat deduces a rule of conduct from the laws of development of society, thus primarily from the class struggle, this law of all laws.... Morality is a function of the class struggle."

Lenin said the same thing:

"We repudiate all morality that proceeds from supernatural ideas or ideas that transcend class conceptions. In our opinion, morality is entirely subordinate to the interest of the class war. . . . Communist morality is identical with the fight for the consolidation of the dictatorship of the proletariat."

When we remember that Lenin and Trotsky felt free to mean by "the proletariat" those proletarians who happened to be conscious of their historic destiny according to Marx, and that these were, broadly speaking, members and adherents of the Bolshevik party, we see the real meaning of this doctrine: namely, that *our party is above moral judgment*. And Trotsky has explicitly drawn this inference:

". . . To a Bolshevik the party is everything. . . . The party is a weapon for the revolutionary reconstruction of society, including also its morality. To a revolutionary Marxist, there can be no contradiction between personal morality and the interests of the party, since the party embodies in his consciousness the very highest aims of mankind."

To call this a belief that "the end justifies the means" is obviously inadequate. It is a belief that so long as our party is, or we can persuade ourselves that it is, a Marxian party of the working class, the decrees of its Politburo transcend all moral as well as criminal laws. For the sake of an *absolutely* blessed social life in the remote future, this conspiratorial organization abrogates those rules of conduct by which humanity—in various ways at various times, but with a growing generality of application—has managed to make possible any kind of social life at all.

Trotsky and Lenin both defend this dialectic Jesuitism by assuming, or pretending, that the only alternative is a belief in "supernatural" or "transcendental" laws of morality. But that only shows that, like all dialectic materialists, they live intellectually in the Germany of 1840. They are blind to the disguised supernaturalism of their own belief. They like to pretend, too, that any who do not believe in this ideological immoralism, do believe that basic social problems can be *solved* by moral exhortation. These two assumptions, or pretenses, have nothing whatever to do with the scientific rejection of Jesuitical ethics.

Morality, to a scientific mind, is nothing but valid practical judgment applied to problems of conduct. Regard for the lives and interests of others occupies, for the reason that man is a social animal, a peculiar position among its counsels. Truth-telling, especially for those who hope that science can solve our basic social problem, is a still more *sovereign* law. Without truth-telling, without a complete, intensely scrupulous and meticulous inward and outward, mental and vocal, integrity, there can be no science. It is primarily this, the most obvious "law" of the laboratory—not any Kantian imperatives or supernatural admonitions of conscience—that a scientific radical would substitute for the metaphysically justified class Jesuitism, and as a corollary, party Jesuitism, of the Bolsheviks.

In his forthcoming biography, Trotsky praises Lenin as superior to his elder brother who was hanged by the tsar, on the ground that Lenin was able to tell a good lie. And he delivers this dictum:

"In spite of the philosophizing of the stern moralists, those liars by profession, a lie is the expression of social contradictions and sometimes also a weapon for struggle with them."

In his congratulation to the Dewey Commission on its verdict of "Not guilty," defending his own good name against a lie, Trotsky expressed the opposite opinion:

"The verdict has an immeasurable political importance," he cried. "The methods of lying and blundering frame-ups which contaminate the inner life of the Soviet Union, and the workers movement of the whole world received today a terrible blow. Let the official friends of the Soviet Union and other pseudo-radical bigots say that the verdict will be used by the reaction. This is untrue. Nowhere and never did the truth serve the cause of reaction. And nowhere and never is progress fed on lies."

A few months later, in his article on *Their Morals and Ours*, he again declared roundly that:

"'Lies and worse' are an inseparable part of the class struggle even in its most elementary form."

There is, of course, no inconsistency here. If one believes in lying as a weapon, one of the most handy, and indeed quite indispensable, weapons would be a lie about that very belief. Trotsky knows quite well that truth has sometimes served the cause of reaction, and progress fed on lies. What he does not know, because no dialectical Jesuit can, is that for large and long-time purposes progress really cannot feed on lies. In feats of social engineering comparable to that indicated in the concept of socialist transformation, honesty and reliable truthfulness, above all in those who lead, are indispensable. This is not a "supernatural law," but a most natural fact. It was well formulated by Goethe, who, scorning such sentimental absolutism as Trotsky's "nowhere and never," declared simply that as between "destructive truth" and "constructive error," the truth, even though destructive, will be chosen by those who are far-sighted:

"Harmful truth is useful because it can be harmful only temporarily, and then leads to additional truths that must become more and more useful; and inversely, a useful error is harmful because it can only be useful momentarily, and then leads to other errors that become progressively more harmful."

The wisdom of this is well illustrated in the sequel to Trotsky's own momentous political lie of October

16, 1926, which spread not only error, but dismay, among his followers throughout the world. During September of that year the oppositional faction led by him had attempted to arouse the worker communists against the strangulation of the Party by Stalin's bureaucratic machine. Believing that the proletarian character of the dictatorship was at stake, as indeed it was, they had gone into some of the great factories in a body—all the big chiefs of the Opposition, Trotsky, Kamenev, Zinoviev, Piatakov, Radek and the rest—to see whether they could rouse the vanguard of the proletariat itself to throw off this bureaucratic incubus that was destroying the revolution. Trotsky never took a more principled and deliberated action in his life. Coincidentally with this revolutionary action—so long and so well prepared that oppositionists in other countries were breathlessly awaiting it—an arrangement was made for the publication throughout the world of the suppressed document in which Lenin himself warned his party against Stalin—the so-called Testament of Lenin.

The appeal to the workers was unsuccessful. The Opposition leaders were shouted down and defeated by the party machine. They did not stand upon their principles and take the consequences while awaiting another opportunity. They offered, as though there were no such thing as principles in the world, to negotiate a peace with the machine. Stalin demanded as the price of peace that they make a public declaration that their action had been unprincipled, a confession that they were guilty of unpermissible violations of party discipline, a summons to their followers to "acknowledge their mistake" and cease all further "factional action," and a promise never to do it again.

Although this belied his principles, besmirched his whole policy, and left his followers out on a limb, and although he knew that in more favorable circumstances he would repeat the attempt, Trotsky submitted to Stalin's demands. He set his own name to the first of those insincere capitulations and false confessions of guilt, which when piled up by that natural process of proliferation which Goethe describes, culminated in the monumental international joint-massacre of truth and the revolution known as the Moscow Trials.*

---

* "We consider it our duty openly to confess before the party that in the struggle for our opinions, we and our followers have in a number of cases since the fourteenth congress taken steps that were a violation of party discipline and transgressed in the direction of factionalism the boundaries set by the party for intra-party ideological struggle. Considering these steps unconditionally mistaken, we declare that we conclusively renounce factional methods of defending our opinions, in view of the danger of these methods to the unity of the party, and we summon to a like renunciation all comrades sharing our views. We call for the immediate dissolution of all factional groups formed around the opinions of the 'Opposition.' We likewise acknowledge that by our actions in Moscow and Leningrad in October [the appeal to the factories] we violated the decree of the Central Committee forbidding discussions throughout the Soviet Union, and that we undertook them against the decree of the Central Committee. . . .. We consider absolutely unpermissible the direct or indirect support of the factionalism of any and all groups in the different sections of the Communist Inter-

Although bogged down and well-nigh buried as a political leader under the weight of these, the legitimate offspring of his own seemingly so useful lie—his stupidly astute deception of the millions of workers and intellectuals who believed in him—Trotsky is unable because of his religion to learn any lesson from it. After seeing the other big leaders of the Bolshevik party come solemnly into court with humanity for audience and deliberately lie the world revolution to death—the most unheroic spectacle to which this sufficiently disheartened modern world has been witness—he continues to sing praises to the heroic super-moralism of the Bolsheviks, and of their prototypes, the Jesuits. The vise that holds him in this mental plight is his belief in class struggle not as a fact of nature, but as a mystic inner dialectic principle, a "law of all laws."

national against the line of the International, whether the group of Souvarine in France, Maslow-Fischer, Uhrbans, in Germany, Bordiga in Italy, or any other group—regardless of their attitude to our opinions. We consider especially unpermissible any support whatever to the activities of persons already excluded from the parties in the Communist International. . . . We express the firm hope that the actual cessation of factional struggle on the part of the Opposition will make it possible for expelled comrades, having acknowledged their mistake in the matter of violating party discipline and the interests of party unity, to return to the ranks of the party; and we therewith promise the party all possible cooperation in its liquidation of factional struggle and its struggle against a recurrence of such violations of discipline."

Signed by Zinoviev, Kamenev, Piatakov, Sokolnikov, Trotsky, Yevdokimov, and published in *Pravda*, October 18, 1926—almost the anniversary of the October insurrection, and by an unhappy chance the very day that Lenin's Testament was given to the world.

THE FACT REMAINS, AND THE METHOD

It will seem to some that in reducing it to fact I have destroyed the force of the class-struggle concept. My belief in it, however, both as a social phenomenon of pervasive importance, and as the basic method of procedure toward a better social system, remains unshaken. If you retain what is really hard-headed in the Marxian system, viewing man's life as primarily the struggle for a living, and not reading any mystic purposes of the universe into that struggle, it is impossible not to see how it has always divided men into classes. It has divided them most significantly into exploiting and exploited classes. Not only Marx, and not only thinkers on the proletarian side, have recognized this, but a whole series of political philosophers from Aristotle and Polybius to Harrington and Locke. As expounded by Harrington, it was adhered to by Alexander Hamilton, James Madison, John Adams, Gouverneur Morris, Daniel Webster. Our American constitution was largely shaped by matter-of-fact men convinced of this fact, and bent on protecting the exploiting classes in their right. I think that those who wish to protect the exploited classes and extend their share in the rights should be equally matter-of-fact.

I do not see how anybody could have watched the career of bourgeois liberal opinion in the United States in relation to the Russian revolution without wishing to dissociate himself from such a record of class-loyal self-deception. If you could plot a curve showing the gradual decline of proletarian class power in Russia from 1917 to 1935, and another curve showing the gradual rise of "sympathy for the Bolsheviks," "support for the Soviets," tolerance of "communism," coquetting with "revolution," in the pages of the *Nation* and the *New Republic,* you would find the curves almost identical. Amid a welter of events and ideas sufficient almost to displace the North Star, these liberal ideologues, while oscillating enough to seem intelligent, have remained pointing along the line of bourgeois class interest with the accuracy of a compass needle. They imagined that in defending Stalin's terrorist liquidation of the Bolshevik party in behalf of a new exploiting class of bureaucrats, they were more "radical" than when they denounced the terror established by the Bolsheviks against the bourgeoisie. They were in the same class position exactly. Although couched in the language of disinterested concern for social progress, their judgments have been loyal throughout to the interests of the possessing classes. The Marxian hard-headedness—the Marxian concept of class struggle made scientific use of—would have made impossible this humiliating record.

I cite this as but one example of the subtle play of class interest. It seems to deserve a position in social and political thinking not unlike that of "libido" in the Freudian psychology. It is not an absolute or universal principle, nor a source or summary of human motives, but its effect when unconscious is so basic and pervasive that it often seems to be. It is in fact, although less absolute, *more* universal than Marx thought, for class divisions, instead of disappearing as he believed they would under collective ownership, seem merely to revert to an earlier form. In typical feudal times the land and labor-power of the serfs belonged first to God, and then to the king, but the lords by virtue of their protective service had control of it. Their right of exploitation rested upon place and function in society, not ownership. It is so with the new class called bureaucrats in the Soviet Union. The industries "belong" to the people, but class divisions and class exploitation are as primitive and brutal as they ever were.

Marx thought he had in the class struggle a dialectical tame beast to ride on into the co-operative commonwealth, but he had a wild leviathan by the tail. Any political animal, if his thinking about politics is to be valid, must have that wild leviathan in mind—the more so, since it is himself. If his social action is to be effective on a large scale, he must take account of it. He must join hands with the class or classes whose broad interest lies in the direction of the change he contemplates.

The tendency of many socialists who reject the dialectic religion and recoil from the Bolshevik fiasco is, while clinging to the extreme aims of Marxian socialism, to go back to the evangelical or utopian method for achieving them. I think we should modify what is still utopian in Marx, the extreme aims, but cling to his practical admonition that they can be achieved only by enlightening economic class interests and organizing them into social and political forces. Undoubtedly the class pattern is more complex than it appears in the Marxian philosophy. It is more complex than it was when that philosophy was born. In particular the problem of the farmer is slighted by the dialectic schema. A new and more statistical approach to the whole question of social dynamics is called for. But it is certain that only those belonging to the exploited classes, or self-identified with them through the vigor of their revolt against injustice and oppression, will have the hardness to go through with any radical program of social change.

13

WHAT TO DO NOW

THE chief trouble on the left is that radicals who have both brains and intellectual honesty have no program. They realize that the Marxian theoretical system is not scientific; * they realize that the application of Marxian practical principles in Russia has been a significant failure. But they do not realize that these two facts pose once more, and fundamentally, the question asked by Lenin in founding the Bolshevik party: *What to do?*

Whatever they do, they will be denounced by the zealots of the Marxian faith and the dupes of the Stalin propaganda as renegades and rascals. They may count on that. And I hope only those inwardly armed against it will entertain the few suggestions I have to make.

The crisis in socialism is partly verbal, as we have

---

* A great many people who remained unconvinced by my writings, have had their eyes opened to the essentially religious character of Marxism by Sidney Hook's recent very brilliant attacks on the dialectic, and by John Dewey's long-awaited pronouncement: "Orthodox Marxism shares with orthodox religionism and with orthodox idealism the belief that human ends are interwoven with the very texture and structure of existence—a conception inherited presumably from its Hegelian origin."

seen, a question of the uncertain destiny of a name. But it has also the substantial problems to solve of substituting science for philosophy, appraising Stalinism as the result of a preliminary experiment, and revising its plan of action in order to avoid another such result.

If I were a more political animal and belonged to a younger generation, I would try to solve all these problems by making the word "radical" mean something— making it mean a new and experimental-scientific movement toward a freer and more equal society. I would not ignore what is to be learned from Pareto's talk about the "circulation of the elite," from Robert Michels's more simply factual and therefore scientific talk about *Political Parties*. But I would regard this, like all valid knowledge, as a fluent aid rather than a fixed obstruction to my purpose. One obvious thing to be learned from Michels is that we ought to be more ready than we are to discard old parties and build new ones. The present situation, it seems to me, calls for a new party, a new press, a new trade union education league, similar in some ways to the old Marxian ones, but based on science and the deliberated experience of these two prodigious decades.

The word "radical" already designates the germ of such a thing. That word has been substituted instinctively in our American speech for the European term "revolutionary"—partly because the latter term is associated for us with a national struggle victorious in the past, but partly also because it is too absolute to describe our attitude to the class struggles of the future. American radicals, like European revolutionaries, want to change the social system profoundly, but on the question how to go at it, their first loyalty is to practical intelligence. If they advocate armed revolution, it is only because that seems a likely method of procedure. In Europe, because of her different history, the first loyalty of anyone wishing to change society profoundly is commonly to a revolutionary tradition. Intelligence has the subsequent function of understanding and guiding a revolution. That, I think, is the significant difference indicated by this change of terms. It makes "radical" an appropriate name for a party wishing to substitute for an imported revolutionary metaphysics the attitude of experimental science.

Such a party would not only "unite science with the proletariat," as Marxists erroneously boasted of doing, but it would strive as a basic principle of its existence to unite scientists with the proletariat. It would not rest its hope essentially, as Thorstein Veblen did, upon an engineering interest in the business system "as a going concern," or advocate the seizure of power by a "soviet of technicians." It would not fail, as the technocrats did, following Veblen, to link up its engineering program with a major social force. But it would recognize the existence and vital importance of that engineering interest, the necessity to the extent possible of uniting it, upon a platform acceptable to them both, with the class interests of the exploited masses.

LIBERTY AND COLLECTIVISM

Such a union would be possible because the party would at last really abandon utopian socialism. I tried in Chapter 9 to identify the utopian elements surviving in Marx's conception of the goal of socialist struggle. I outlined in eight propositions the changes that it seemed to me a practical mind would make. In particular, I pointed out that in linking up individual liberty with co-operative production by the state, for no better reason than their faith in the benign intentions of a German universe, the socialists have made a capital error.

This error, brought to such white light in Stalin's tyranny, might be epitomized in this way: Marx pointed out that with the development of capitalistic factories, production had become a co-operative process, but ownership had remained individual and private. All you have to do, he said in effect, is to socialize *ownership*, and you have the free and equal society. It seemed almost as simple as removing the lid to get at a nicely prepared pudding. What he failed to note was that with the development of factories production had become a co-operative process *under a factory boss.* When the lid was removed, the boss was found to be the most prominent thing in the pudding.

There is no use wishing away this disappointment with arguments about Russia's backwardness, as the Trotskyists do. It is not Russia's history, but man's nature, the nature of co-operative production, that is in question. Trotsky's attempt, while denouncing the result of his seizure of power in Russia, to assemble the masses for another seizure on exactly the same terms in Spain, collided with the intuitive good sense of mankind. The socialists are not much more convincing when they insist that only the tactic of Lenin and Trotsky, only the *Bolshevik application* of Marxism, was an error. The feeling of a free mind is that if co-operative production failed to liberate anybody in Russia but the boss, there is something wrong with co-operative production as a means of liberation. Until that something is frankly faced and corrected, no socialist party can appeal strongly to either critical intelligence or intuitive sagacity. The Stalinists, who make no appeal to either, will suck the masses in with their Russian fables and rabid totalitarian passion to the movement toward another tyrant state. Unhappily many earnest socialists will abet them in this fell purpose, believing their crass fables only because there appears no other clear alternative but to abandon the whole Marxian idea.*

A new radical party, or any preliminary group looking toward the formation of such a party, would have to confront this question frankly: How far is liberty to be sacrificed to co-operation, how far co-operation to liberty?

Having insisted for well-nigh a hundred years that all our democratic freedoms are but an incidental product of the free market demanded by capitalist production, it is time for socialists to ask: Will not those freedoms disappear, then, if you abolish the free market? If the primary interested activities of men are economic, must they not, in order to be free, be free in those activities? Can you eliminate classes through state action without suppressing the natural impulses of mankind? And will

* A tragic example of what I mean is Upton Sinclair who, after devoting a life's labor to the struggle to give the world's riches to the common man, finds himself in advancing age defending the most ruthless, bloody and systematic armed assault on the common man, the most wholesale governmental torture and massacre of those very same simple, hard-working men, women and children who are the heroes of his passionate novels, that history will perhaps ever record.

A year ago Sinclair proposed "one simple method, as certain as litmus paper in a test tube" to determine whether the Soviet Union is counter-revolutionary: "When Hitler learns that the Soviet Union has become counter-revolutionary, he will reduce the ardor of his crusade against it . . . when that happens I will admit that Stalin has sold out the workers."

Since then Hitler has joined Stalin in a military pact, but Sinclair is still unable to make this admission. I think it is because he has the intuitive good sense to know that it entails an admission about socialism itself. It necessitates a reconsideration of the doctrine to which he has consecrated his life, and he is too tired to undertake that job.

not these impulses, denied expression in private enterprise, find inevitable expression in the creation of a state bureaucracy which exploits the working class more efficiently than the private capitalist can? Such questions can no longer be dodged.

Stalin has abolished the free market—he has abolished capitalist competition—and the other freedoms have disappeared. They have disappeared so completely as to leave no hope that the *oppressive* aspects of capitalist economy can also be abolished: control of the means of production by privileged classes, and exploitation of the workers through the wage system for the benefit of those classes (what Marx called surplus value). In making the total mechanism of such exploitation a state monopoly, Stalin has given a power to those who constitute and run the state, such that a restoration of elementary popular rights can hardly be thought of except in terms of democratic revolution. Am I wrong in thinking that an unacknowledged consciousness of this fact is what is killing the socialist movement in other countries, while the so-called "communists," who accept the hideous outcome and go in for totalitarianism in its most savage form, are able to grow and flourish? A radical party, at any rate, would have to acknowledge and confront such facts.

BEWARE OF TOTALITARIANISM

It is beyond my scope to draw up the economic program of such a party. Unfortunately I can only describe in very general terms the position which I think it ought to occupy. I do even this with diffidence, for of the two main ingredients of wisdom, practical action and detachment, I have for some years cultivated only the latter. Still it seems obvious that any new program to replace Marxism, if it is scientific, will be, like other achievements of modern science, a social product. And I do not see how it will be arrived at, unless everybody who recognizes the need tosses in what ideas he has with a certain friendly abandon just as they have formed themselves in his mind. My main contribution—or at least the one most difficult to bring out of my mouth—would be this word of prudence about communal ownership.

I think that a scientific radical party will have to abandon the casual assumption, based, after all, only upon Christian ethics and the analogy of the family, that complete collectivization is the obvious foundation for a more general enjoyment of life and liberty. Seeing what has happened in Russia and the fascist states, it will proceed cautiously with the experiment of collectivization—not out of timidity or tenderness toward the possessing classes—but out of a realistic regard for its own purpose of genuine emancipation.

It would, to begin with, marshal the proletarian class forces behind some such program as that which Max Lerner calls "democratic collectivism," envisaging a society in which "private property and private industrial initiative would remain; but the capitalists could make their decisions on policy only within a frame-work set by planning boards." It would assert, as Lerner does, that a democratic capitalist society *can* plan, "if the majority and its leaders have the courage to take capitalism away from the capitalists, and make its basic decisions socially rational and responsible." But it would be wary of that "planned socialism" to which Lerner regards such a blessed state-of-things as but "a transition step." For he is willing to give this same name, "socialism," to Russia's systematic exploitation of the workers through the wage system and the totalitarian state. He is willing to believe that the profits of the advancing industries of that military bureaucracy, although at the disposal of a monolithic minority party assumedly composed of human beings and not angels, are nevertheless graciously distributed among the working classes. His indifference both to facts of human nature and to statistics indicates that his thinking here is directed, not toward changing the world, but toward acquiring comfortable emotions about its future. It is ideological thinking—always to be watched for when a soft-headed liberal goes in for the "iron mood."

A radical party, if it has the character I am advocating, will have none of that indifference, and none of that soft-headedness. It will cherish real values and cherish the working classes. And I for my part am convinced that, in so doing, it will find itself increasingly skeptical of that "complete collectivization" which these same liberals are now so blandly adopting as their own. It will re-examine all the dissident socialist doctrines—syndicalism, guild socialism, libertarian communism, the co-operatives, production for use, etc., in search of guarantees against the totalitarianism which now seems inherent in state ownership. Unburdened of the delusion that a new day is dawning in the East, it will turn its eyes to the North, to Sweden and the other Scandinavian countries, where a good deal of daylight seems to have been shining for some time on social problems. It will study both the remarkably humane and democratic civilizations achieved there, and the role played by class forces in the process of their achievement.

It will be alert also to the many new ideas that are coming to birth now that Marxism has ceased to be the preoccupation of a few rebels, and is actually being mastered and criticized with sympathy by the best-trained minds we have. I call attention especially to Eduard Heimann's *Communism, Fascism or Democracy,* a profoundly thoughtful book, proposing changes in the socialist ideal based upon "the principle of having the pattern of social and property organization correspond to the pattern of work." Heimann's bold confrontation of the problem of agriculture, so fatally pushed aside as incidental by the dialectic philosophy, his substitution of "parity" for "equality" in the concept of a just society, are original enough to have marked a decade in the old socialist thought. While such ideas are coming to birth, there is no reason to despair of the inventiveness of the race. It is only necessary to have a political organization with an experimental platform, a platform open to receive them.

A radical party ought to have its own Institute of Social Research and Invention, a committee of its best minds, some of them—and pray God not all!—professional economists, subsidized for the task of devising ways to overcome, without totalitarian control, the basic fault in capitalist production, its incapacity to distribute the abundance which it has made available.

The problem is to find some method by which society can induce, with a continuous rhythm and on a basis of increased production, that adjustment between production and purchasing power which the New Deal has tried to induce in desultory spasms, and with a restricted production.* It is no doubt a more intricate problem than it seems to one remote from business enterprise, but it ought not, once it is clearly defined, to transcend the inventive genius of mankind.

Had Marx himself realized that his economics was a demonstration of the impracticability of a matured capitalist production, he could hardly have failed to raise the question: Is there no way, without sacrificing the benefits conferred upon mankind along with the free market, to mend this flaw in its operation? Marx believed, as we have seen, that he was discovering contradictions in capitalism, indicative of the manner in which a dialectic universe was in process of supplanting it with something better. That is another way of saying that his first loyalty was to a revolutionary tradition. Anyone whose first loyalty is to practical intelligence will, at least with the results of the Russian experiment before him, instinctively raise that question. And a radical party, as I conceive it, will have to provide some answers. It will have to propose American experiments, based on the real truth in the Marxian analysis of capitalism, but not

* As a man called in to cure the mortal disease of democratic civilization, President Roosevelt will go down to future history—if history has a future—as a horse-and-buggy doctor, humane, sagacious, helpful in an emergency, but technically untrained and inadequate. In particular his attempts to correct a condition arising from overproduction in relation to buying power by cutting down on actual production, will be dismissed as an amateurish therapy not dissimilar to bloodletting.

deluded with the metaphysical false hopes inherent in the Marxian dogma of communal ownership.

To some this will seem, I suppose, equivalent to an abandonment of socialism, but that ought not to worry the coming generation. What we want is a movement of hard minds, loyal to the oppressed, disillusioned as the socialists are of moral and rationalistic evangelism and of self-consoling ideologies, but instructed as they are not of the errors as well as the truths in Marxism, and able to learn all the lessons of the Russian revolution and the fate of the Third International.

INTELLIGENT INTERNATIONALISM

Such a movement would think differently about internationalism and the peace-and-war problem than socialists have. They have followed Marx in his peculiar blindness to the existence of nations—his theoretic habit, rather, of regarding nations as a part of what is "given" to the historian, like the earth itself upon which history happens. This enabled Marxists to explain international wars as wholly due to economic causes, and to dismiss all modern wars, without specific investigation, as "imperialist"—as squabbles, that is, about colonial empire. That was a reckless oversimplification of the truth. But even where it might exhaust the truth, it would not exhaust the problem of what attitude toward a war actually in progress a radical ought to take. That is a question, not of causes, but results. Lindbergh has informed us, much in the spirit of his socialistic father, that the present war in Europe is not a struggle for democracy against totalitarianism, but merely a "struggle for power." Suppose that that statement, when broken down into its constituent specific meanings, proved entirely true. It still might be true that upon the outcome of this war depends the question whether democracy is to survive in Europe or not. The battle of Marathon was a struggle for power, and Marxians would have little difficulty in showing that it was also a struggle about colonies. But nevertheless upon the issue of that battle depended the survival of the Athenian system of democracy.

I myself think that every effort should be made to keep the United States out of the present wars. The geographical and economic accidents which make possible a complete experiment in democratic civilization on this continent are the most precious thing left to the human race. If while they fight, we can solve the problems about which they are fighting, we shall have fulfilled our highest destiny. In general, however, I think we must—at the cost of a good deal of smart-alecky satisfaction—abandon the Marxian oversimplification of war's causes, and learn also that when a war has begun, its causes are a secondary question. Practical thinking should then concern itself with results.

WHAT TO DO NOW

We must be more realistic also about the problem of war's prevention. The notion that "the workers have no fatherland" and that once the private capitalist is got rid of, nations will spontaneously merge together in a universal brotherly society, seems so obviously utopian now that one can hardly believe it ever formed a part of "scientific socialism." Here again it was left to future history to resolve with rainbow work the conflict between freedom and union, individuality and co-operation. With nations as with people that is the essential problem. The best that can be hoped for—or indeed desired by those still interested in the colors of life—is a federation of obstreperously patriotic nations exercising real police power through the world. That, however, is a vital necessity, and to postpone working for it on the ground that a proletarian revolution is going to hand it to us on a silver platter, with the dying away of the state and the end of "barrow-pushing as a profession," is sheer mystic folly. Intelligent socialists have already pushed this dream into the shadowy portion of their minds; a scientific radical movement would push it out altogether.

REFORM AND REVOLUTION

A party taking the lead of such a movement would fight honestly and whole-heartedly for measures of social reform, regarding even a temporary prevalence of more civilized conditions as a good in itself. But it would stress the distinction between those measures which constitute a fundamental gain by the lower classes, and those which are an effort of the ruling classes to sugar-coat the process of exploitation. It would be in that sense a party of revolutionary progress.

To safeguard such progress, as well as for their own sake, it would defend wherever and to what extent these exist, the laws and institutions, and above all the social habits, of democracy. It would oppose in all republics the attempt, whether calling itself communist or fascist, whether masquerading as democratic like the Stalinists, or openly advocating dictatorship like the Trotskyists, to build a dual power with a view to substituting in a crisis the sovereignty of a party for that of the state.

A revolution in the true sense, however, a nation-wide collapse of government and a spontaneous uprising of the masses, cannot be simply advocated or opposed. Such an event, like a tidal wave, would carry any real workers' party with it, whether as a guide or on the tow-line.* The present attitude of revolutionary Marxists is to regard the struggle of the working class to better its conditions under capitalism merely as a preparation for this assured event. As Rosa Luxemburg expressed it, "The struggle for reforms is the means, the social revolution

---

* "A revolution cannot be made to order—it grows. . . . If the objective conditions change an uprising is inevitable."—Lenin in 1917.

the aim." And this general idea has given rise in all socialist platforms to a sharp distinction between "immediate demands" and "ultimate program." A party recognizing the limits of scientific knowledge, recognizing that a proletarian revolution may or may not come, and if it comes, may or may not succeed, would abandon this equivocal attitude. It would struggle for reforms with unmixed motive, but would also make known its proposed line of conduct in a revolution. Instead of dividing its platform into "immediate demands" and "ultimate program," working for one and keeping the other half-way up its sleeve, it might, it seems to me, draw up a "program of radical reforms" and a "program of action in a revolution," and lay them both on the table.

For the latter program, it might borrow from the original constitution of the Soviet Republic. In that document the principle of "proletarian dictatorship" appears in the only form in which a prudent mind will ever again approve it, as a limitation of the franchise to those who do not exploit the labor of others. An experiment with such a government, a genuine workers' and peasants' republic, is still to be tried. For the Soviet government was from the first, as Trotsky himself has frankly revealed, something in the nature of a hoax. The popular belief that any real power resided in the supreme organs of that government he has recently described as an "optical illusion." While the "population," he says—or should we translate it *populace?*—was diverted by this optical illusion, "the principal questions, the discords and conflicts were resolved in the Politburo [of the party] which from the beginning played the role of a super-government." *

That super-government was the germ of Stalinism, of fascism, of Nazism. The Soviet government had it governed, the Soviet constitution had it become the law of the land, might conceivably have put Russia in the lead of the movement toward a more genuine democracy. Had it perished in the attempt, the leadership in an ideal sense would still be there. A super-government of true believers in the historic destiny of the proletariat, as expounded by Karl Marx and interpreted by themselves, is not a workers' government, and to one who understands as a natural fact the role played by class in human history, holds no hope of a step forward toward such a government. With every recognition of their high sincerity in making it, this mistake of the Bolsheviks, in which their mystic faith upheld them, would

* "These two figures [Kalinin and Yenukidze] incarnated the supreme Soviet organs in the eyes of the population. On the surface the impression was created that Yenukidze held a good part of the power in his hands. But this was an optical illusion. The fundamental legislative and administrative work was done through the Council of People's Commissars under the leadership of Lenin. The principal questions, the discords and conflicts were resolved in the Politburo which from the beginning played the role of a super-government." (*New International*, April 1939.)

be regarded by a party basing itself on a scientific conception of the class struggle as a betrayal both of science and of the proletariat.

FLEXIBILITY AND THE PRESENT MOMENT

The chief affirmative lesson to be learned from Lenin and his adaptation of Marx and Hegel is that of mental flexibility without moral compromise. Lenin himself exclaimed in a marginal note made when first studying the dialectic philosophy: "Flexibility, flexibility to the point of conceiving everything as turning into its opposite—that is the practical meaning of the dialectic." *
If actually carried to that point, flexibility would be tantamount to manic incoherence; but in the dialectic philosophy a corrective is provided by the "upward" course of all these otherwise bewildering changes, and by the fixed goal to which the material forces were conceived to be proceeding. Lenin's full meaning was: "Flexibility as to the course to be taken toward a goal fixed in general terms by the nature of the matter in process of change."

It is not an incidental joke on Marx and Hegel that their so motionful and fickle worlds proceeded with constant purpose toward a single goal, and when they got there stopped. It is the essence of their philosophies both as wish-fulfillment systems and as guides in thought

* Quoted from memory.

and action. The goal of the universe was really the wish and purpose of the man within it. In Lenin the inflexibility of this purpose, its absolute sovereignty among his motives, was quite as marked as his flexibility of mind. Combined with an extraordinary scope of intellect, and a rare sense of the specific relations between means and ends—a gift that glorified the name of common sense—these two traits substantially define his genius.

We have to learn this art of flexibility, and learn to manage it without the wish-fulfillment system. This means that we have to be more flexible, not less so, than Lenin was. He realized that his goal was fixed only in general terms—"None of us knows what socialism will be like when it arrives," he used to say—but for us those terms must be still more general. We can no longer even be sure of the economic set-up implied by the term socialism. We have changed "the society of the free and equal" to "a freer and more equal society"—a very fundamental change. And in other ways, while transferring the socialist purpose back from external matter into our own minds, we have generalized it. We have become more subject to the stubbornness of facts. We cannot believe that the world is going toward our aims when it is not.

In a little while the negative part of what I am saying here will seem academic and superfluous, because the immaturity of the Marxian system will be obvious when looked back at. But it will always be important to hold to this valid principle of flexibility, the sense of operating in a process, the habit of inventing new ideas, new slogans, new organizations for new conditions, which distinguished Lenin from all other political leaders. And it is important right now to realize that he did not carry it far enough.

All Lenin's policies after 1917 were based upon the premise that "this is the period of the breakdown of capitalism," and that socialism must sooner or later replace it. We do not know what "period" this is, and cannot know until we look back from a chosen point of view. Nor do we know whether capitalism—which suffers from the frailties of all abstract nouns—is breaking down, nor what is going to replace it. We are deprived of all those fixed points.

We know, it seems to me, as surely as we know anything, that the present general mode of production and distribution has become inadequate, and that some thorough-going repair-work or reorganization is in order. We know that in the process of that reorganization the free and democratic institutions which have developed under the present set-up are in peril. The smallest germs of democracy have disappeared through half the world. In the other half they are under insidious attack. Democracy is on the defensive.

That, I think, should be the general premise underlying the present-day policies of any political organization that is radical in the sense in which I use the term. And if we are flexible in the Leninist and super-Leninist sense—if we have learned the most vital lesson in the whole Marxian lucubration—we shall not hesitate to proclaim this fact, and act accordingly no matter what bulls to the contrary may be issued by the orthodox High Priests. Democracy is on the defensive; that is the primary fact. Any offensive operations now undertaken must have in view, as of prior importance, the strengthening of the defense. Any operations endangering the defense must be deferred.

CONCLUSION

It may seem utopian to hope that a militant party, or any insurgent social movement, can be organized on a platform of scientific good judgment. It is hard for enthusiasts to remember the limits of knowledge. It is hard for crusaders to know that their crusade is an experiment. It involves—especially if one comes to this mature position from the Marxian left—a task of emotional reorganization. The task, however, can easily be exaggerated by wrongly educated intellectuals. American labor has fought hard, and at times violently, without any faith or philosophy but hard common sense. The scientific attitude is closer to this fighting common sense than any philosophy ever was or will be. To teach scientific method to a working class, especially an American working class, is simpler and more natural than to bring to it, by means of a pseudo-materialistic system of wish-fulfilling metaphysics, a "consciousness of its historic destiny." The very virtue of a *class* struggle is that it does not require to be fanned up and sustained by super-factual ideologies. The zealots, the doctrinaires, the neurots in search of a religion, have this need, but not the workers, not the engineers. For them the facts are enough.

That the formation of an experimental scientific party should be an experiment is fitting. If such a party has to remain for a long time, or even permanently, an affiliated section of a looser and less expert mass party, that does not make the need of it less urgent. The idle youth of this period of depression are in search of a standard to rally round, a crusade, a consecration. In the absence of an affirmative program from the honest and intelligent radicals, they are falling for the half-dumb and the demagogues who disguise under any plausible ideology the grab for totalitarian power. They are going over to Stalin and Hitler by default—learning to denounce factual good judgment as "defeatism," praise bull-headed self-delusion as "grim determination," call blind political passion "realistic," and bigotry in the service of established power "objective." They are making these fatal errors because we offer them nothing to do. We fail to make the path of honest intelligence a path of consecration, of sacrifice, of heroic effort. We fail to make it grim. We fail because we have no name, no press, no organization and no affirmative program. But that is an accident of the historic moment. It is not inherent in the nature of scientific intelligence.

INDEX

Adams, John, 239
Agriculture, collectivization of, 43, 44
Anabaptists and Diggers, 190
Anglo-Russian Committee, 111
Anti-intellectualism, 84-85
Aristotle, 239
Arnold, Thurman, 212
Assignment in Utopia, 179
Atlee, Clement R., 158

Beal, Fred E., 179; quoted, 183
Beard, Charles, 212
Bicameral system, 35
Blue-prints for new society, 175
Bolshevik party, foundation of, 101
Bolsheviks, clean-up of, 34
Bordiga, 238
Borkenau, F., on the Comintern, 101, 110, 114
Brandler, 108, 109
British Military Socialism, 159
Browder, Earl, 116
Bukharin, 57, 107, 203
Bulgarian party, 110
Bulgarian uprising, 111
Bureaucracy, organized, 32
Bureaucrats, 241

Calvinism, 168
Central Committee, Resolution of, 68

Centralism, 124
Chamber of Deputies, march on, 114, 115
Chiang Kai-shek, 112
Chinese revolution, 112
Class struggle, doctrine of, 215-242
Classless society, defined, 36
Comintern, the, outline of, 95-119; story of, 101; organization of parties, 102; detachment of, 103; Stalinism, an outgrowth of, 104; fascism, a by-product of, 104; history of, 105-119; second congress of, 105; rightward turn of 1921, 106; second rightward swing of, 111; left swing of, 112; the Popular Front slogan, 115; and the Spanish revolution, 115-116; Fourth Period of, 116
"Communist," change in meaning, 30-32
Communist International, history of, 105-118
Communist party, 33
Communist Youth, reorganization, 34
Confessions, Moscow, 63-66, 77-79
Constituent Assembly, dissolution of, 101

Constitution, under Stalin, 34, 35
Co-operative Commonwealth, 198-199
Cowley, Malcolm, 17
Crowther, Geoffrey, quoted, 91

Darwin, Charles, 178
Decree on Academic Reform, 21, 22
DeMan, Henry, 212, 213
Democratic collectivism, 250-251
Denny, Harold, quoted, 42
Dewey, John, quoted on schools, 17; on orthodox Marxism, 243
Dictators and Democracies, 50
Dies Committee, the, 137
Differential rewards, 37-51; *New Republic* on, 38, 39; Soule on, 38; comparison of, in Russia and America, 38-40; Wilson on, 39
Diggers, 190
Discussion of Human Affairs, The, 212
Distribution of income, 37-51
Divorce, 24
Drucker, Peter, quoted, on public lying, 79
Duranty, Walter, quoted, 31

Economics, discussed, 47-51
End of Economic Man, The, 149
Engels, Frederick, quoted, 204
Escape, penalty for, 27
Esthonia, *Putsch* in, 110

Fabians, 137
Family relations, 23
Farrell, James T., 185
Fascism, comparison with Stalinism, 82-94

Fascism, description of, 149
Fechner, Gustav, 178
Fischer, Louis, 33
Fischer, Ruth, 109
Flexibility, mental, 261-264
Foster, William Z., 96, 97
Fourier, F. M. C., 176
Fourth Period of the Comintern, 116
Frank, Waldo, 17
Free market, the, 248, 249
French Teachers' Federation, 29
Fuehrerprinzip, 125
Führer, the American, 158
Fülöp Miller, René, 194
Funk, Dr., 126
Future of Liberty, The, 140

German communist party, 113
German revolution, failure of, 109
Goebbels, 126
Goethe, quoted, on lying, 235
Gold, Michael, 136
Goldman, Albert, 35
Gorky, Maxim, 17

Hamilton, Alexander, 239
Hamilton, Cicely, quoted, on sex and family relations, 25
Hannibal, life work of, 211, 212
Harrington, James, 239
Hegel, Georg Wilhelm Friedrich, 67; metaphysics of, 32; philosophy of, 164
Hicks, Granville, quoted, 41
Historic mission of workers, 220
Hitler, Adolf, accession to power, 113
Hook, Sidney, on dialectic, 243
Hoover, Calvin B., quoted, on economics, 50-51

INDEX 269

Howard, Roy, 115
Huxley, Aldous, quoted, on drugs used in Moscow Trials, 74; revolutionary metaphysics of, 178

I Was a Soviet Worker, 179
Ideology and Utopia, 212
"Immediate demands," 259
International, Red Trade Union, 111
International, Second, 25; Third, 25, 26
Internationalism, in new party, 255
Izvestia, 29

James, C. L. R., quoted on Leninism, 104, 105; on Brandler, 108, 109; on Esthonian *Putsch,* 110, 111
Jeffersonian ideal, 191-192
Jesuitism, 229-230
John Reed, the Making of a Revolutionary, 41

Kalinin, Michael, 136, 260
Kamenev, 73, 236, 238
Kapital, Das, commentator of, quoted, 200-201; discussion of, 207-209
Keep America Out of War, 156
Kent, Rockwell, 17
Krestinsky, 72, 73
Krivitsky, on Moscow Trials, 78
Kulaks, expropriation of, 43, 44

La Follettes, the, 112
Laski, Harold, 17
Leader, the, in Russia and Germany, 84
League for Peace and Democracy, the, 137

Left, defined, 118, 119
Leftism, in America, 116
Lenin, quoted, on Third International, 26, 27; government, on schools, 21; attack on Stalin, 33; revolutionary theory, 60; Testament, 64-66, 236, 238; last speech to International, 99; book, *What To Do,* 101; *State and Revolution,* 103; warning against leftism, 112; speeches and articles, quoted, 131-132; on individuality, 145; on objection to socialism, 153-154; quoted, on readiness for revolution, 186; writings, expressions in, 193; on higher social forms, 210, 211; on creation of working-class ideology, 216; on the state, 228; quoted, on lying, 232; as liar, 234; on revolutions, 258; lesson to be learned from, 261
Lenin, Mme., quoted, at funeral, 134
Lerner, Max, 251
Ley, Dr., 157
Libertarian radicals, 144-146
Lincoln, "bourgeois" theory of, 192
Lindbergh, C. A., 256
Literature and Revolution, 127
Litvinov announcement, 25
Locke, John, 239
Loyola, Ignatius, doctrine of, 230, 231
Luxemburg, Rosa, 220-223; quoted, on Social Democracy, 221, 222; on reforms and revolutions, 258, 259
Lying, party, 66-68; discussed, 229-239
Lyons, Eugene, 179

Madison, James, 239
Mannheim, Karl, 212
March of Fascism, The, 91
March on Chamber of Deputies, 114, 115
Marx, Karl, 17; ideologies defined, 17; solution of economic problem, 138; philosophy of, 164-167; quoted, on social transformation, 173-174; quoted, on Paris Commune, 174; on integrating man, 176-177; on barrow-pushing, 189; phrases revealing goal, 189; on political power, 190; on history, 197-200; on the class struggle, 215
Marx and Lenin, 212
Marxian Socialism, restated, 169-170; theory of Soviet system, 59; theory summarized, 165-166; world-view, truth in, 197-209; theory of history, 199-200
Marxism, of Soule, 140-143; Bolshevik application of, 247
Maslon, 109
Mdvani, Budu, 56
Mensheviks, 59, 61, 171
Monolithic party, 83
Morality, discussed, 229-239
Morris, Gouverneur, 239
Motive-patterns of Socialism, 126-148; libertarian socialists, 129, 131, 132; gregarian socialists, 130
Moscow Trials, 52-80; victims of, 55-58; confessions, 63-66, 237-238; torment used in, 71; drugs used in, 74
Mrachkovsky, investigation of, 77
Muralov, 56

Narodnaia Volia, 100
Nation, The, 139
Nationalization of industries, 151-153
New Deal, the, 116, 253
New radical party, outline of, 251-264
New Republic, The, 139
New society, blue-prints for, 190

OGPU, the, 69, 71
Old Bolsheviks, Society of, 34
Oppositional faction, 236
Ostrogliadov, salary of, 40, 41
Owen, Robert, 176

Party, single, in Russia and Germany, 83
Party lying, 66-68
Patriotism, in Russia and Germany, 83
Peasant Government, Stambouliski's, 110
People's Front, in Spain, 59, 60, 61
People's Will, the, 100
Personalities, role of, 210-214
Piatakov, 56, 236, 238
Pilnyak, income of, 42
Pilsudski, 112
Planned economy, 137-138
Politburo, 232
Political tyranny, 28-35
Polybius, 239
Popular Front, 115
Pravda, quoted, on motherhood, 23, 24; on Third International, 26
Prevention of war, 257
Profit Motive, The, 137
Proletarian Journey, 179
Psychology of Socialism, The, 212
Public lying, 76-80
Putsch in Esthonia, 110

INDEX

Radek, Karl, 55, 101, 236
"Radical," new meaning of, 244
Radical party, outline of new, 251-264
Rashenbush, Stephen, quoted, 91, 92; *March of Fascism*, 229
Rauschning, Herman, 149, 157
Realpolitik, 139
Real Situation in Russia, 33
Red Trade Union International, 111
Red Virtue, 33
Reed, John, 41, 55
Reform, social, under new party, 257, 258
Religion, in Russia and Germany, 83, 84
Revolution Betrayed, The, 43
Revolution of Nihilism, The, 149
Right, defined, 119
Rights of Man, 139
Rolland, Romain, 17
Roosevelt, F. D., 116, 254
Rousseau, J. J., 167
Russia Twenty Years After, 179
Russian communist party, 95

Saint-Simon, C. H. de, 176
Schools, under Lenin, 21; changes in, under Stalin, 21
Second International, the, abandoned, 25
Sedov, Leon, quoted, 38, 39
Serebriakov, Leonid Petrovich, 55, 56, 76-77
Serge, Victor, 179
Silone, Ignazio, quoted, 131
Since Lenin Died, quoted, 32, 33; Lenin-Stalin fight, 65
Sinclair, Upton, 248
Smith, Andrew, 179; quoted, 182

Social Democracy, 110
Social fascists, 113
Social Myth, the, 212
Social Patriots, 113
Socialism, end of, in Russia, 17-50; abandoned for communism, 25; defined, 36; beneficiaries of, 44, 45; motive-patterns of, 128-146; predicament of word, 149-160; suggested adoption of, by England, 159; as philosophy, 161-172
Socialist, change in meaning, 30-32; ideal, the, summed up, 195-196; revolution, union of Stalinism and Nazism for, 158
Society of Jesus, 230
Society of Old Bolsheviks, dissolution of, 34
Sofia, cathedral of, blown up, 111
Sokolnikov, 238
Sorel, Georges, 212, 213
Sossnovsky, 57, 58
Soule, George, 17; on differential rewards, 38; quoted, on beneficiaries of socialism, 46; on liberty, 140-143
Souvarine, Boris, 179, 238; quoted, 183
Spanish revolution, 115
Spencer, Herbert, 178
Stakhanovist Movement, Sedov on, 38, 39; new caste, 43
Stakhanovists, earnings of, 43
Stalin, 179
Stalin, on armament, 25; and agricultural problem, 43, 44; and the counter-revolution, 52-80; establishment of democratic government, 60
Stalin-Hitler pact, 81, 157
Stalinism, comparison with fas-

cism, 82-94; description of, 150-151
Stalinists, in America, 230, 231
Stalin's revenge, 74, 75; perfect day, 76; statement to Roy Howard, 115; totalitarianism, 153
Stambouliski's Peasant Government, 110
State, theory of the, 227-229
State and Revolution, 103
Strong, Anna Louise, 33, 42, 194

Technocrats, 245
Testament of Lenin, 64-66, 236, 238
Theft, death penalty for, 28, 29
Third International, 95
Third Party of the Bourgeoisie, 111, 113
Third Period, civil war, 112, 113
Thomas, Norman, quoted, 156
Thomism, 168
Totalitarian liberals, 139-143
Totalitarian state, change to, 34; state-capitalism, 137
Totalitarian State of Mind, 140
Trade Union International, 106
Treason, escape crime of, 27
Trotsky, Leon, quoted, on differential rewards, 43; on treatment of leaders, 97, 98; on Lenin, 120; quoted, on dogmas of Bolshevism, 121-123; quoted, on ruthlessness, 126; quoted, on new society, 127; on personality, 145; on betrayal of the revolution, 162, 184, 185; *Problems of Culture*, 193; on Spanish revolution, 225-226; quoted, on lying, 231, 232, 234; signatory to confessions, 238
Trotskyists, 34; treason plot, 62
Twenty-one Points, the, 105, 107
Tyranny, political, 28-35

Uhrbans, 238
Ultimate program, 259
Ultra-rightism, period of, 116
United-brotherhood movement, the, 134-137
United Front, the, 106, 107
Unitéisme, 176

Vaksov, Victor, 42, 43
Veblen, Thorstein, 245

War, prevention of, 257
Ward, Harry F., 137
Webb, Beatrice and Sidney, 17; quoted, on inflation, 47
Webster, Daniel, 239
Weltanschauung, 157, 168
Wilson, Edmund, quoted, on differential rewards, 39; on communism, 138
Wilson, Lucy, quoted, on schools, 20, 21
Winter, Ella, quoted, 33
Wolfe, Bertram D., 156
Women, position of, under Stalin, 23
Workers' Democracy, 32
World Revolution, 104
Writers, position of, 37
Witherspoon, Mrs., quoted, on victims of Moscow Trials, 73

Yenukidze, 260
Yevdokimov, 238

Zinoviev, 73, 107, 110, 236
Zinovievists, 34

For Product Safety Concerns and Information please contact our EU
representative GPSR@taylorandfrancis.com
Taylor & Francis Verlag GmbH, Kaufingerstraße 24, 80331 München, Germany

www.ingramcontent.com/pod-product-compliance
Lightning Source LLC
Chambersburg PA
CBHW070557300426
44113CB00010B/1287